NON-FICTION

133.9013 OL4c

Oliveira, Jacquelyn Frances
Case for life beyond death

DISCARDED
by the
Mead Public Library
Sheboygan, W.

WATER DAMAGE

W9-ADT-150

1/01   9000866901

THE CASE FOR LIFE
BEYOND DEATH

JACQUELYN FRANCES OLIVEIRA

William Laughton Publishers
Elm Grove, Wisconsin

All possible care has been taken to trace the ownership of every selection that is copyrighted and to make full acknowledgement of its use. If any errors have inadvertently occurred, they will be corrected in subsequent editions provided notification is sent to the publisher.

Excerpts on the following pages have been used with permission:

All scripture quotations, unless otherwise indicated, are taken from the New King James Version. © 1982, Thomas Nelson, Inc. Used by permission. All rights reserved.

Pg. 1 reprinted with permission of Bantam Books from *tuesdays with Morrie* by Mitch Albom © 1997.

Pg. 13 reprinted with permission of Doubleday, a division of Random House, from *Death By Choice* by Daniel C. Maguire © 1988.

Pg. 14 excerpted from *God In All Worlds* by Lucinda Yardey (ed), reprinted with permission of Pantheon Books, a division of Random House © 1995.

Pg. 40 reprinted with permission of C.R. Gibson Co. from *The Healing of Sorrow* by Norman Vincent Peale © 1966.

Pg. 43 reprinted with permission of DeVorss & Co. from *As A Woman Thinketh* by Dorothy J. Hulst © 1910.

Pg. 45 reprinted with permission of Simon and Schuster from *Unlimited Partners* by Robert and Elizabeth Dole © 1988 by Robert and Elizabeth Dole.

Pg. 52 reprinted with permission of Simon and Schuster from *Intangible Evidence* by Bernard Gittelson © 1987.

Pgs. 58, 117–20 excerpted from *Parting Visions* by Dr. Melvin Morse and Paul Perry. © 1994 by Melvin Morse, M.D., and Paul Perry, reprinted by permission of Villard Books, a division of Random House, Inc.

Pg. 60 reprinted with permission of Simon & Schuster from *The Journey Home* by Phillip Berman © 1996 by Phillip Berman.

Pgs. 66–67 reprinted with permission of Crystal Cathedral Ministries from *Positive Encouragement for You: 365 Promises of Hope From the Heart of God* by Dr. Robert Schuller © 1988.

Permissions continued on page iv

THE CASE FOR LIFE BEYOND DEATH © 2000 by Jacquelyn Frances Oliveira
William Laughton Publishers, P. O. Box 588, Elm Grove, WI 53122-0588
All rights reserved. No portion of this book may be reproduced without written permission from the author.

ISBN 0-9674041-0-X
Printed in the United States of America
First printing: January 2000

Editor: Chris Roerden
Assistant Editor: Elizabeth N. Hoffmann
Cover Designer: Mary Beth Salmon

Publisher's Cataloging-in-Publication

Oliveira, Jacquelyn Frances.
    The case for life beyond death / Jacquelyn
Frances Oliveira. -- 1st ed.
    p. cm.
    Includes bibliographic references.
    ISBN: 0-9674041-0-X
1. Immortality.   2. Future life.   I. Title.
BL530.O45 1999   218
                    QBI99-1345

866901

DEDICATION

This book is dedicated with great love to:

William J. Downey
> for the depth of his spiritual vision
> and his faithful friendship

Rudolph E. Morris
> for his wisdom and courage
> and his spiritual kinship

Frank B. Oliveira
> for his care and confidence
> and his spiritual transformation

Permissions continued from page ii

Pgs. 71–72 reprinted with permission of Celestial Arts from *On Life After Death* by Elizabeth Kubler-Ross © 1991.

Pg. 74 reprinted with permission of Twayne Publishers from *The Essential Swedenborg* by Sig Synnestvedt © 1970.

Pgs. 79, 175–78 reprinted with permission of Patricia Treece from *Messengers: After-Death Appearances of Saints and Mystics* © 1995 by Patricia Treece.

Pg. 85 reprinted with permission of Simon & Schuster from *A Believing Humanism: My Testament 1920-1965* by Martin Buber © 1967.

Pg. 97 reprinted with permission of The First Church of Christ Scientist from *Science and Health with Key to the Scriptures* by Mary Baker Eddy © 1934 by Mary Baker Eddy.

Pgs. 100, 109, 203, 204 reprinted with permission of National Christian Education Council, 1020 Bristol Rd., Selly Oak, Birmingham, GB, B29 6LB, from *Life Begins at Death* by Leslie D. Weatherhead © 1969.

Pg. 107 reprinted with permission of Word Publishing from *Angels: God's Secret Agents* by Billy Graham © 1975.

Pg. 107 reprinted with permission of Honor Books from *John Wesley's Little Instruction Book* © 1996.

Pg. 111 reprinted with permission of Celestial Arts from *Grist for the Mill* by Ram Dass © 1988.

Pgs. 123–24 excerpted from "The Reality of the Spirit," by J.B. Phine, with permission of *Guideposts Magazine* © 1963 by Guideposts, Carmel, New York 10512.

Pgs. 125–26 reprinted with permission of Viking Penguin, a division of Penguin Putnam, from *The Medium, The Mystic, and The Physicist* by Lawrence LeShan © 1966, 1973, 1974 by Lawrence LeShan.

Pgs. 128, 144–45 reprinted with permission of Ariel Press from *After We Die, What Then?* by George Meek © 1987.

Pgs. 134–35 reprinted with permission of Edgar Mitchell from *Higher Creativity: Liberating the Unconscious for Breakthrough Insights* by Willis Harman and Howard Rheingold © 1984 by Edgar Mitchell.

Pg. 145 reprinted with permission of Morton Kelsey from *Afterlife: The Other Side of Dying* by Morton Kelsey © 1979.

Pg. 151 excerpted from *With the Tongues of Men and Angels* by the Institute of Noetic Sciences © 1992 by Holt, Rinehart and Winston, reprinted by permission of the publisher.

Pg. 160 excerpted from After Death Communications by Lóuis LaGrand © 1997 Llewellyn Worldwide Ltd., P.O. Box 64383, Saint Paul, MN 55164.

Pgs. 160–61 reprinted with permission of Bantam Books, a division of Random House, from *Hello from Heaven* by Bill and Judy Guggenheim © 1996.

Pgs. 163–64 excerpted from *A Grief Observed* by C.S. Lewis with permission of HarperCollins Publishers, Inc. © 1961 by N.W. Clerk.

Pgs. 170–71 reprinted with permission of NavPress from *Your Work Matters to God* by Doug Sherman and William Hendricks © 1987.

Pg.188 reprinted with permission of Little, Brown & Co. from *How To Meditate* by Lawrence LeShan © 1975.

Pgs. 188–89 excerpted from *Surprised by Light* by Ulrich Schaffer reprinted with permission of HarperCollins Publishers, Inc. © 1980 by Ulrich Schaffer.

Pg. 197 reprinted with permission of Simon & Schuster, from *People of the Lie* by M. Scott Peck, M.D. © 1983 by M. Scott Peck.

Pg. 199 reprinted by permission of Morehouse Publishing, Harrisburg, PA, from *The Dark Face of Reality* by Martin Israel, M.D. © 1989 by Martin Israel.

CONTENTS

ACKNOWLEDGEMENTS

I wish to thank those who read parts or all of the manuscript for their encouragement, generosity, and commentary: Mr. Frank Zeidler, Dr. Phil Zweifel, Dr. Harvey Berg, Dr. Scott Stoner, Chaplain Dave Hanser, Kitty Clark, Janice Paral, Mary Lorch, Chuck Heinrich, and Mike Andrews.

I wish to express my appreciation to my editor, Chris Roerden, for her encouragement and objectivity.

I wish to express my gratitude to my cover designer, Mary Beth Salmon, for her integrity and support.

I wish to also thank my secretary, Brenda Dugan, for her enthusiasm and patience in taking on and completing this new project. I wish also to thank Diane Dalhoe, Tom Riegert, Joyce Travis, Donna Albrecht, and Betty Gygax for their unfailing cooperation and good will.

Jacqui Oliveira

PREFACE

Let's begin with this idea," Morrie said in *tuesdays with Morrie.* "Everyone knows they are going to die, but nobody believes it."[1] Technology today makes it possible for some to carry this to an extreme. Consider, for example, a slogan associated with the Life Extension Society: "Freeze, Wait, Reanimate." This society provides its members with a "freezer card" that will admit their bodies at death into cold storage until medical science can cure their diseases and bring them back to life. Relatives of the deceased members of this society are allowed to view the frozen bodies of their loved ones by means of closed-circuit television.

Our contemporary society is rich in traditions and offers each of us a multitude of illusions, compromises, and distractions. How are we to make sense of our deepest feelings, our most piercing questions and engaging experiences? How are we to choose whom to trust, what to believe, and for what purpose?

Not a day passes that I fail to have contact with

intelligent people with inquiring minds and sensitive souls seeking meaningful spiritual experiences and confirmation in their relationship with God, with the Divine. Not a day passes that I fail to be in contact with truly precious people seeking to glorify God and express joy and creative thinking in their complicated daily lives. Each day I am in contact with death and bereavement at some level. I am no stranger to trauma, tragedy, sorrow, disillusionment, and despair. I feel pain acutely. I sense the devastation and bewilderment of those I counsel, teach, and love. I know their struggle and their search for new meaning, deeper reality, and hope reborn. I appreciate their hunger for the sustaining presence and power of God, their longing for a taste of eternity for themselves and some experience of their departed loved ones. I admire their courage and tenacity, and I admire their respect for the tenets of transformation.

I witness firsthand how personal lives can be disrupted when people are drained by grief and intimidated by the arrival or circumstances of death. I feel the energy and passion diminished in their family life, work life, and community life. I understand that many of these people lead very active lives and do not have time or resources for discerning study. Often they are uninformed and can be misguided easily by infor-

mation that is inadequate or seductive. Sometimes
these people are frustrated by narrow, rigid religious
pronouncements and judgments that often leave them
uninterested, alienated, and—at times—even hostile.
Sometimes these people are the recipients of superficial psychic explanations, which, in the long run, leave
them empty and dependent.

How, then, do we integrate the life and love of God
within our own human journey? How do we integrate
eternity and death, our human experiences, and
experiences with those on the other side of earthly life?
How do we integrate our faith tradition, intelligence,
and personal experiences in our relationship with the
Divine?

In light of these questions, I will attempt to convey
a composite view of my own spiritual journey, the
deepening of my faith in God and eternal life, the
expansion of my awareness, the discoveries in my
before-death and after-death experiences, and the
revelations and insights developed in me through
these years and experiences.

It is my intention as I write this book to nourish
and awaken you on your own journey. I hope you will
find clarification for your own thoughts and percep-
tions in these vital and sensitive areas of life, death,
eternity, and faith. I hope what you read confirms

some of the experiences you have had with your loved ones who have died and gone on ahead of you. I hope, too, that new growth will be stimulated, as well as a willingness on your part to seek God and the eternal in new and deeper and higher ways. In addition, I hope you will find support for yourself, where you find yourself at this point in your life.

I encourage you also to feed on the bibliography in your own continuing search and understanding. Doing so will provide you with supportive material and new information that can help you to understand and clarify even further all that I share with you in this book. Culturally, we are a people accustomed to instant gratification. Yet when we seek answers to questions that are eternal, when we seek to immerse ourselves more fully in the spiritual life and the spiritual world, it is not possible to do so quickly or without effort. Discernment is required on the part of every authentic seeker.

I did not come into this area of investigation overnight. It has taken me many years of a very intimate search and communion with God. What I share with you in this book follows thirty years of in-depth bereavement counseling and death education. It has required of me a great deal of research, openness, and personal sacrifice. This really is no different for those with whom I work or meet regularly—precious people who have an authentic commitment to living productively and peacefully on this good Earth. In some cases these are people who have a growing awareness of and participation with those they love who live in the world beyond. In some cases these are people who recognize themselves as children of God, led by the Spirit of God, reflecting God's Life, Love, Light, and Truth. All are precious people who seek to understand more of the reality of after-death experience and after-death communication—precious people who seek to know more of the spirit world beyond the Earth.

INTRODUCTION

In writing this book I have tried to create a pathway for you related to the meaning and value of death experiences. I felt it was important to lay the groundwork in general, and treat several aspects of this subject in particular. This is a book that invites you to ponder and return again and again to some of its images and ideas. As you read, memories of your own will surface. Perhaps you will gain a truer appreciation of those memories. Questions will be stimulated, and you will desire to read additional material about what calls you forward.

Some of you might be just beginning your own spiritual search. Please be patient with yourself about the feelings and questions that emerge. Some of you may be well along on your spiritual journey and able to identify comfortably with this material. Please find validation for yourself in that awareness. And, some of you might be beyond what you find here, yet you are able to appreciate what is expressed and how far you have come personally. Please honor that.

Decidedly, this book is an affirmation of God and of eternal life. It is an affirmation also of who we are as human persons on Earth and who we are called to be as spirit persons throughout all of eternity.

Throughout this book I try to bring several themes together. But you need to make connections of your own between what you read and what you have experienced, hope to experience, and perhaps have yet to experience in your own lifetime. Each of you needs to consider all of this in light of your personal faith life, religious tradition, relationship with the Divine, and experiences with your dear departed loved ones.

Therefore, may I encourage you to try to find the presence of the Divine and more, not less, of who you are in all of these experiences: near-death, dying, deathbed visions, mystic visions, apparitions, and after-death occurrences. I encourage you to develop your own spiritual gifts and talents, as well as your psychic abilities, for the glory of God and the benefit of humankind in this world. I further encourage you to be serious-minded, not superficial, and discerning, not naïve. That is not easy, it seems to me, in a society where distractions are legion. Cultural rewards and enticements are real, omnipresent, and seductive, even if they are only temporary. It takes wisdom and maturity to reach out and hold on to the eternal. The world is steadily shouting at you to let the eternal go, and the world will promise you an easier way, a more exciting way. I myself have never been able to think clearly, feel deeply, or see very far when there is too much noise or too much haste or too much waste. I have always known that I wanted to hold on to the eternal. I have always tried to reach out for its splendor, wonder, excellence, and beauty.

CHAPTER ONE

FINDING MEANING IN DEATH EXPERIENCES

A s Americans, we enjoy a world of abundant good living, promising us stimulation, satisfaction, happiness, and accomplishment. Our gods are many and competitive: pleasure, power, progress, prestige, and wealth . . . to name a few. Our goals are often grandiose and lofty. My observation is that too many of us don't know when we reach a goal because we've been busy setting so many new ones along the way.

Information explodes around us, continuously; opportunities are new everyday. In the minds of many, bigger is better. Success and glamour entice us wherever we seem to look. Image-making is big business.

Titles define us and technology connects us.

We are a society on the move, competing, winning, exploring, and designing people, products, plans and places. We are in control. We take charge and make things happen. We work to be free and unencumbered.

The media sets social standards and formulates social agendas for us, and we compare ourselves, our lives, our purposes accordingly. We are face to face each day and evening with the entertainment and sports industries, and their gods and goddesses "living the good life." Politically and economically, we see much being rewarded that is not worthy. Often, the only reality check people know and accept is what they see passing before them on the screen and in the marketplace.

Our personal and social value is often determined by the money we make and spend, the celebrities we know, and the appearance we present. Who we are, what we believe the purpose of life to be, for many often comes prepackaged and preapproved. However, this purpose endures for such a short span. New trends, new fads, new demands produce change, and we conform again, temporarily. Our lives and our sense of self seem to lack unity and real purpose.

As we make our way forward, however, we begin to encounter other sides of life—disappointments in

love, frustration in work, betrayal in friendship, failures in family life, impaired health, not enough money,
not enough fun, feelings of emptiness and alienation.
Add to this trauma and tragedy.

Many of us, however, are not contented living in
the fast lane, feeding on what shouts loudly and
moves quickly. Some of us inhabit other worlds, some
of us look within ourselves to reach outward again
with greater meaning and effectiveness. Some of us
find satisfaction in quiet service to others, in simple
pleasures and delights, and in study, silence, and
solitude. Some of us find joy in developing our creativity. Some of us find a sense of mastery in cooperative
enterprises. Some of us seek excellence in and for
family, church, and society, based on enduring values
and commitments. Some of us value our ethical and
moral development. Some of us ponder deeper realities and pursue higher purposes. Some of us see with
more penetrating vision the world of people, the world
of creation, the world of Spirit. Some of us are restless
enough to ask more perceptive questions and to reject
social hypocrisy and self-deception. Some of us reject
the allure of excess and strive to balance the many
forces within ourselves and within the world. Because
you are reading this book, I suspect that you are one of
these people: uncomfortable with illusion and willing

to try to understand deeper realities. If so, you will want to consider carefully the following question. Why is it important for us to talk about death and dying?

As Americans, we take great pride in being a progressive people. Yet the irreversible fact of death causes us to feel impotent in the face of this reality.

Our reaction to death is usually determined by our expectations of life, the meaning we attach to the ending of life, and how we cope with losses. The Dalai Lama says, as *A Policy of Kindness* reports, "If you are mindful of death it will not come as a surprise—you will not be anxious. You will feel that death is merely like changing your clothes. Consequently, at that point you will be able to maintain your calmness of mind."[1]

In his book *Living With Dying,* Glen Davidson writes "If we expect life to be unending, then dying seems to be an illusion. If we believe life is vocation, then dying is an intrusion, if life is a threat, then death is an escape, if we accept life as a gift then dying is part of the given."[2] We pay a price, however, for denying or neglecting our relationship to death. It is so intimately interwoven with life. When Sogyal Rinpoche, the acclaimed spiritual director, first came to the West, he was stunned to find such a difference between the attitudes toward death he encountered and those he had been raised with.[3]

In spite of the wide array of western scientific and technological achievements we, in the West, seem to have little grasp or deep comprehension of death or after-death experiences. Rinpoche observes that there is scarce meaningful attention or dialogue given to the process of dying. In ordinary conversation the topic is virtually ignored. If it is included it causes some irritation or embarrassment. When westerners engage in such conversation it is usually pessimistically, superstitiously, or jokingly.

In his book, *Death By Choice,* Dr. Daniel Maguire writes that only in a mature culture can death come of age. If a people or culture do not value maturity, it will not be easy to receive and accept death as a natural companion of life. In western culture we try to ignore and deny limits and boundaries. We are action oriented and seem almost addicted to power. "Small wonder," Maguire comments, "that western culture has been so slow to come to grips with death, which is, after all, the very ultimate in passivity, impotence, and limit."[4]

I have the opportunity to move in many circles of society, religious as well as secular, and I am amazed, so often, at how many intelligent and goodnatured, committed people believe that this human life experience of ours is all there is, that death means annihilation or loss. I am saddened by their impoverishment, their lack of vision, and their lack of awareness of ultimate meaning.

Death denial is a form of numbing that tends at many levels to limit our capacity for feeling, vitality, passion, and creativity in many other areas. In this sense, confrontation with death is not only a means of clarification, but also a source of life and direction and commitment.

J. Krishnamurti once wrote that "Death is always there watching, waiting. But the one who dies each day is beyond death."[5]

As maturity invites us to grow beyond appearance and superficiality and move toward a deeper, more embracing understanding of death, I believe we begin to value life and death more consciously as a process and an awakening to more meaningful opportunities.

Death, then, can be considered as a point in a process . . . a point of change in a process of experience. Life is filled with little deaths and necessary losses. As we move through these transitions and stages, we have the opportunity to mature and gain perspective at many levels. In this sense we die each time we encounter our boundaries and change, and we live more fully each time we surrender to reality and are transformed by its truth and meaning. Life and death are related to our identity. From birth to death, we struggle to die to our false self and faithfully claim or become our true self, our real self, our eternal self.

Seen in this light, dying can be an awakening to greater opportunities. It invites us to reexamine our values, rearrange our priorities, rededicate our life's mission, cherish self-care and the care of others. It helps us to refuse to waste living on this good Earth, refuse to be affected by the pettiness of others, refuse to give in to toxic relationships and defeating behavior. It encourages us to value life's pleasures, to celebrate life as a gift, to enjoy and delight in beauty. It invites us to live in the present as fully as possible, to choose to grow in love and wisdom, and to seek and know and serve the God of our being and eternal destiny, with a sense of pleasure and wonder.

At the same time, families can grow closer when they are able to open to each other's questions, vulnerabilities, faith experience, and hopes, and communicate about the reality of their own deaths. Friends share precious moments when they can laugh and cry and plan together. Communication and dialogue help each of us affirm and experience the continuity of life here on Earth and life unfolding eternally.

It seems to me that in a culture such as ours, so self-indulgent and "now" oriented, we have a passionate need to proclaim the wisdom and beauty of all that is eternal, again and again and again.

It's helpful for each of us, in unique and practical ways, to talk more confidently with those we love about the lessons we have learned and failed to learn in our earthly journey. It's also important to decide on the messages, gifts, and taped videos we wish to leave with those we cherish. Doing so facilitates healing for our grievers at a later time. It is also helpful to arrange the kind of funeral or memorial service we prefer to have for ourselves. It is a magnificent act of consideration for others and an affirmation of our own faith in the purpose of life and death. All these efforts require courage and dignity and give meaning to who we are. All our insight and commitment nourish who we are as we continue to grow, develop, and communicate after we die, as we consciously live on eternally with the God of creation and redeeming, steadfast love.

When we look more closely at the death experience itself, we see that it can do many things for us. What lessons does death teach us? Fifty million people die every year throughout the world.[6] They leave the Earth and move on to live in eternity. I will be one of them someday and so will you. I am looking forward to participating in the Divine life that awaits me, to enter more fully into new learning and growth. But for now, I am fully committed to my life here, and whatever I experience of the death reality comes through the experience of those I love and with whom I work.

I wonder if you have ever seen another person die. I wonder if you have shared in the death of someone you loved and cared for deeply. I wonder how you feel about this.

Death can be personally transforming in the sense that we realize at the most intimate level we are a part of a continuous life. Ten years ago, I sat at the bedside of the mother of one of my sixth grade boys. Beth was dying of lung cancer. She was one of the most beautiful and creative women I had ever known. The depth of love and commitment she expressed through her life for her husband and son moved me profoundly. We talked of the plans she had made for them, the hopes she had for them as they would continue in life, the dreams they had already realized together. In her life and in her dying, she brought joy, courage, and empowerment to them and so many others. Her religious faith was steady and radiant.

Today her son, Jeffery, is in graduate school preparing for a career in counseling. Her husband, shortly after her death, entered the field of nutrition and health. Both of these men reflect her optimism and courage and have the wonderful capacity to affirm

others. They were tested painfully early in life, but
they feel they are enriched today because of their early
experiences with death. Beth taught me that in the
long run, no effort is ever wasted, and that we must
plant seeds generously and trust them to grow.

I wonder if you know of anyone whose life has
been transformed by the death of another. During my
undergraduate days in college, one of my closest
friends, Kathleen, watched her dearly beloved grandmother die suddenly and without warning. As she
looked on, feeling helpless, she decided silently to
become a medical doctor. Against many obstacles, she
fulfilled her promise, in honor of the love and confidence her grandmother had expressed to her all
through their life together. Kathleen was changed
deeply by this loss; I saw that in her immediately.
Through the years, I witnessed how she has been able
to bring healing and hope to so many wonderful
people because of the meaning she derived from her
early experience with sudden loss.

In death, we become aware there is a real opportunity for ourselves and others to demonstrate love,
forgiveness, gratitude, and faith in ourselves, in each
other, in the Spirit of God, and in eternal life.

Nearly two years ago I experienced the unexpected
loss of William J. Downey, the president of our com-

pany. Bill was a favorite of mine, dear to my heart and a colleague whom I held in the highest esteem. We worked closely together on designing all of our educational programs. He had a keen interest in the afterlife as well. Bill was faced with a five month debilitating struggle with pancreatic cancer. Just two weeks before he died I taped my farewell message to him, sending it on to him by mail, for his heartfelt reflection.

Dear Bill,

When I arrived here at my office today, I received my copy of the letter you wrote to us announcing your retirement as President of Wisconsin Memorial Park. I took a long time to read your letter reflectively, and I was filled with many mixed emotions. Understandably, it must have been a very difficult letter for you to write. A turning point for you, a very difficult turning point. Your letter was written to signal your departure from a place and world you loved so dearly. I know it required much of you, not only in its composition, but by everything you poured into it . . . all the meaning it held for you and all the meaning it holds for all of us here.

In the minds of all of us, your inspirational leadership was a potent force in building a quality product and a quality reputation. Forty-five years of service and vital leadership gave you an incredible combination of experiences. I know you learned many enriching lessons and made some remarkable contributions. Please continue to take pride in that.

I'm sure that everyone will be telling you, in his or her own way, how much they will miss you. I, too, surely will miss you, miss you far beyond measure. I recall when you hired me. And I recall all that you did to foster the programs that were so unique, first and foremost to Wisconsin Memorial Park owners, but also to the entire Milwaukee community. Please be assured that our programs will continue with dedication and excellence. You were truly a pioneer. You truly had a sense of vision, and I applaud you for that.

I believe that these last five months of your life have been a testing time for you at many levels. I'm sure that you have realized some valuable personal lessons. Some of them, are known to you and easily understood, accepted and integrated in varying degrees. Others are not so easily known or understood. I'm sure that you must feel, at one level, confused and resentful, hurt and angry that you could not complete your work at the Park in the manner that you desired. You gave so completely and so carefully to your work, and you exercised your leadership with dignity. You left your office believing you would have the opportunity to return and do things your way, that you would return to facilitate your retirement when the time came. I am very sorry that you did not have that particular opportunity.

I do hope this does not embarrass you, but in some way, I think you share a kinship with Moses. We read in the Bible that after all of his tireless work, he was not able to enter the promised land. He was able to see it, but not enter it. God had other good and important things in mind for him. God has other good and important things in mind for you. You are ready for these discoveries and gifts . . . some of which you know and some of which remain divinely mysterious to you. God is able, God is trustworthy, God is intelligent and creative. God understands and accepts you just as you are. All of these things you know.

Over the last three and a half years, we have had so many profound discussions, and I value every single one of them. In some ways, in addition to being my employer, you were also a mentor to me. I'm glad we were able to share so widely and authentically about life and death and eternity as growth experiences. Every day, in some way, growth happens. You are open to this. You know and believe life is everlasting. The passage of time, and circumstances you find yourself in right now, contain many hidden messages.

These are possible because you have had to undergo deprivation, frustration, pain, immobility, and deep disappointment. No man relates easily to these hardships, to the ugliness of pain and dependency. It feels to me unfair. At a human level, it is unfair. But it is also a prelude to so much more. You know that. I know that.

The people around you know that. Your family knows that.

So I do thank you, Bill, for the letter you sent. I will keep that letter for a very long time. Each day, in some way, I remember you in prayer, and I recall in various ways all the kindness you extended as we worked together. Thank you for your confidence in me. Thank you for your foresight in pioneering the grief education program which brought help and healing to countless numbers of people. Thank you for making it possible for me to share with you my personal experiences in life, death, eternity, and with God. Thank you for the realism you offered and the maturity, talent, and dignity you brought to our relationship and the work we did. Thank you especially for being you and for your nourishing friendship.

Thank you for your Christian commitment and for your steadfast faithfulness to God. I have so many memories, they will nourish me for some time to come. I know that you were proud of all that was accomplished, and that makes me proud also. I know that you have a commitment to your God and God will truly honor that. You have made it possible for light to shine on this Earth. You will continue to experience and express more of the Divine light as you move forward.

As you so well know, we do not have to understand to believe, but we must trust the goodness of God. God is willing and God is able to guide you all the way and complete your story. You have many answers yet to be revealed to you. That has to be encouraging.

It has been a privilege to work and learn with you. May you willingly, humbly, and confidently embrace now, all that the Prince of Peace has especially for you.

Fondly,
Jacquelyn

The loss of Bill Downey at work was a quiet, painful awakening and a deep personal struggle for me. In the weeks and months following Bill's death I learned to exchange his active, creative leadership, refreshing spontaneous humor, and supportive personal dialogue. What emerged slowly was a spiritual, intuitive relationship, invisible to my eye, but intimate within my heart. In that exchange, I was changed dramatically.

When you part from your friend, you grieve not
For that which you love most in him may be
clearer in his absence, as the mountain climber
is clearer from the plain.

The Prophet—Kahlil Gibran

The beauty and wonder of nature seemed to soften that transition for me somewhat. Quiet walks by moonlight, early morning prayer, scriptural readings, meditation by the lake, and a Wisconsin weekend drive through Door County providing a visual feast—

were all supportive. The music of Brahms and
Debussy was soothing for me, and reading my poetry
offered inspiration. Through my days of grief, visits
with my young godchildren brought laughter and
spontaneity, and I was once more planning sweet
surprises to add variety to their days.

Soon thereafter, as night turned into day, I reached
for my pen. My column "The Healing Heart" would
soon be due. I found myself writing "When Change
Comes Into Our Lives—What Meaning Does It Have?"

The human experience of daily living carries with
it changes of great magnitude and lesser magnitude,
but always, in all ways—change comes to each of us.
Sometimes change provides clarity and new opportunities for us to reflect once more, and to reorganize and
redirect our energy, our trust, our confidence and
hope. Sometimes these changes create chaos and
confusion, stimulate fears, and give birth to bewilderment, leaving us empty and feeling forlorn.

When our relationships and routines change
through death, our longings for love and security
linger. When our life responsibilities dissolve or
double, we often feel drained and devastated. Change
comes with or without permission. As it must, change
seeks to be embraced and honored over time. It often
feels like an enemy and adversary rather than a com-

rade and friend. Change must be taken seriously, if not appreciated. It helps us realize that all we shared for a time was wonderful, stimulating, and safe. Change invites us, somehow, slowly, to integrate some of those blessings into our present realities of living. It helps us to recognize what was deficient and burdensome and to release what no longer is appropriate, adequate, or necessary.

Change tempts us to regress and clouds our vision, obscuring present possibilities. Change requires courage—the capacity to move ahead—in spite of despair, doubt, disappointment, and dread. Change requires new energy and the willingness to take risks, to try again, to cooperate, to reenter life in a different way, to experience relationships and activities from a different perspective.

Change requires patience and perseverance. Change is a part of a continuous cycle. Change asks us to learn larger lessons in life beyond appearances, beyond what can be immediately understood and explained. Change humbles us as easily as it enlarges us.

Change is a process inviting us forward. God is in change. God is a supportive resource for us through our changes, revealing more of His/Her grace and fidelity and intimate knowledge of and personal care for each of us. We are changed by change, and with courage and faith we can be transformed in healing ways by God's grace, transformed to live our lives with appreciation for who we are now and for the days and months ahead of us.

Death is perhaps one of our most personal and intimate experiences. It connects us with our deepest inner self; often it connects us to others, family members, and friends in very deep abiding ways.

Thirty years ago I sat for days in the hospital room of one of my most beloved college professors and a cherished friend, Dr. Rudolph Morris. In those days, I witnessed Rudolph's courage and humility, generosity, wisdom, and profound Christian development and faith. His spiritual gifts seemed to flow out from him to me, empowering me and preparing me for many of life's challenges, then unknown to me, but awaiting my response, ahead of me. I felt deeply the transforming presence and power of the Holy Spirit during those days and nights, through so many of Rudolph's questions, shared stories, and ideas. Rudolph's dying days proved to be teaching days for me. Together we entered into a gentle dialogue. We shared the darkness together, respecting its silence and its sadness.

His plain and simple hospital room became holy ground. He continued daily to reach out to many of his beloved friends and colleagues whom he called to his bedside, imparting blessings that left them with messages of wisdom and love. These messages were affirming and liberating, allowing their recipients to demonstrate more of God's life in ever new ways in their individual lives and development.

Fifteen years later when my lovely friend Peg, a nurse, was dying, I spent several hours with her in her peaceful hospital room. We talked softly about her needs at that time—her family, her longing for God, her emptiness, and her fulfillment through her life. I felt deeply her need for comfort and beauty in those moments. Yet, I felt inadequate and somehow unsure.

The next evening, after sunset, while I was deep in thought and meditation, I had a very beautiful and profound experience of Mary of Nazareth. I experienced her profound and tender love, her deep peace and compassion, and her exquisite, exquisite beauty. When she came, she contained me in all stillness. She enveloped me with her completeness and her grace. She came in darkness but she felt as light. I did not know her before this, and with this experience of her— her comfort, her intimacy, her full and maternal love and support—I felt a new awakening, a new call, a new bonding. New contentment, wisdom, and love unfolded within me.

Within a few days I returned to the hospital to visit

Peg, knowing it would be the last time for us here. She
was ready to move on. I sensed in her a new peacefulness and confidence. She sensed in me a new joyful-
ness and fulfillment. We were able, in our own special
way, to encourage each other onward—she heaven-
ward, me earthbound. Somehow I no longer felt
unsure and inadequate. I could see that Mary's love
had freed me and filled me in a new way, so that I
could now overflow into other lives more securely.

Death also separates us for a time from those who
love us and from those we love. That separation makes
it possible for greater growth to unfold within us and
for us to participate in a greater and glorious life plan.

Death allows the Divine the privilege of guiding us
further along to greater life and love and truth as a
part of our eternal journey . . . allows God to unfold
within us a greater sense of our own being.

Biblically, in the Judeo-Christian tradition, we have
many assurances of God's graciousness and of Divine
wisdom. In Ecclesiastes 3:11 we read, "God has made
everything beautiful in its time. Also He has put
eternity in their hearts." Each of us has been given a
deep desire for and awareness of our eternal home
deep within our being. As we live our lives God uses
many means to awaken and cultivate this wondrous
gift.

Again we are reminded of God's everpresent faithful love.

In Jeremiah 23:23–24 we read:
> Am I a God near at hand
> And not a God afar off
> ... Do I not fill heaven and earth?

We find ourselves cherished by God when we read in Isaiah 49:15:

> Yet I will not forget you. See, I have inscribed you on the palms of My hands.

That comes back to say to us that we are in intimacy with a God who cares deeply and passionately for each of us.

Jesus tells us in John 14:18: "I will not leave you orphans. I will come to you." And he does . . . over and over again in the course of our earthly lives, offering us support, strength, hope, and healing. Again, Jesus reminds us in John 16:22: "You now have sorrow, but I will see you again, and . . . your joy no one will take from you." He will call us by name as we make our transition because He knows us, and we will recognize His call as Master because we know His Spirit. And again Jesus promises us in John 14:2: "In my Father's house are many mansions . . . I go to prepare a place for you." Many of us take great pride in that relationship with Christ and find complete comfort in His profound and reliable promises to us. Finally, in Psalm 90:12 we read: "So teach us to number our days, that we may gain a heart of wisdom." Here we are encouraged to appreciate the supreme value of wisdom in living our lives to the fullest.

In all of the major religions wisdom is a cardinal virtue, and it is clear to me that our eternal journey is a heart journey as well as a head journey. It is good to remember that our hearts are involved in trying to understand and appreciate this eternal journey. I want to encourage you to "listen" to your heart concerns as you make your journey and to resist the temptation to make eternal reality a "head trip." So, too, it is helpful not to get lost in an intellectual discourse or debate that alienates the Spirit of God and enthrones only the human ego and/or the human intellect. So much of the contemporary literature and thought does that. I find so much of what is available irreverent, and, I must admit, irrelevant.

Even the most serious-minded and authentic thinkers and disciples among us are grossly inadequate to cover a subject of this magnitude. I am not adequate to do so. Many are not adequate to do so. But this must not prevent us from making a beginning and contributing to the exploration and understanding of the journey as we know it. It must not prevent us from contributing to the discussion as we are called to do so.

Therefore I invite you again to reflect on what is offered here, in light of your own search and personal experiences and faith life. It seems to me very important that you learn to treat your experiences and your questions as sacred. Allow them to design a beautiful pathway forward in your spiritual life and relationship with the Divine. Allow them to awaken and refine your relationship with yourself and others. Allow them to help build a bridge between life, death, and eternity.

The eternal journey is a knowable one, but it is still a mystery, and I feel sure that each of us, in good faith, will be more pleasantly surprised when we actually enter into God's Light more fully.

I believe it matters enormously to God that we treat this search with care and competence. I am not in agreement with those who believe it is enough that eternity will take care of itself. How we come to understand ourselves spiritually, what we choose to develop in ourselves spiritually, what we come to understand of reality, and how we invest our energy and purpose has merit not only on Earth but also when we pass over. It is more important that we personally seek, reflect, digest and discover more of eternity for ourselves.

CHAPTER TWO

EGO GROWTH AND SOUL GROWTH

I t is of no minor consequence how we are shaped and conditioned by the culture in which we are born and live. Admittedly, culture is a rich and persistent force in shaping attitudes, values, beliefs, and behavior. American culture is multifaceted; it is rational, scientific, progressive, materialistic, affluent, technological, secular, humanistic, and youth oriented. Today, we find ourselves living in a postmodern, information age.

All of these facets permeate how we think, what we believe, what we expect from life, and what goals we strive to achieve. Many Americans, if asked what they hold dear, as social goals would include living a good, comfortable, successful life, and having a loving family, a successful career, a happy retirement, and a college education for their children.

Americans likewise take pride in their psychological awareness and goals. If we are to be healthy and autonomous, it is necessary for us to develop a strong managing ego, to be in control of our life circumstances, to be competitive, and to win. We strive also to be good decision makers, to achieve recognition and success, to discover cures, to solve problems, to realize our fondest dreams. We find strength in learning how to negotiate effectively and to make reasonable judgments.

In this society, logic and science are gods. We revere these channels for approaching and knowing reality. It is through science that we are directed to find our answers. We seek also to be as fully conscious as possible. We seek to know and understand ourselves, each other, relationships, and political and economic processes. Our energy from birth onward is used to expand our awareness, to take charge, and to become responsible.

Culture also affects our attitudes toward death and dying. In spite of some of the progress we have made, we are still, by and large, a death-denying culture. Death and dying do not fit neatly into our American way of life. Death is frustrating, it stops things, it causes pain. Sometimes it's embarrassing, in light of our success history and command performances.

If we shift now from this level of analysis to consider a higher, more embracing level psychologically and spiritually if you will—our focus is directed differently. I invite you to consider carefully the following words:

JOURNEY   TRANSFORMATION

PROCESS   GRACE

I suggest that each of us is on an inner journey, one of purpose, preparation, change, and development. We are also on an outer journey, one of activity, accomplishment, enjoyment, power, and responsibility. Essentially, as many see it, our human journey is one of faith and love and wholeness. Our journey is a transformational one. "Transformational" implies in a sense that where we find ourselves at one point, how we come to know ourselves and life, should not be where we find ourselves or how we come to know ourselves and life at another point. Our transformation admits to various degrees and operates at many different levels—some known and clear, some unknown to us.

This transformational journey involves process—that is the movement and use of our energy through time, energy that shapes and directs and empowers us in life. Dr. Elisabeth Kübler-Ross refers to this process at an image level, contrasting the caterpillar with the butterfly. It seems to me that this is a good image, worthy of our time and reflection.

In what way do you become the butterfly through human life? In what way do you move from dependence to independence, brokenness to wholeness, bondage to freedom, stagnation to creativity? In what way do you move from hurt to healing, bitterness to forgiveness, and foolishness to wisdom?

Many events in our lives serve as a catalyst to activate this process. Crisis, pain, disease, change, injustice, discrimination, betrayal, and death are powerful agents. Promotion, success, financial reward, true love, political power, harmonious relationship, sexual fulfillment, mystical experience, and joy are likewise significant. All of these have the potential to move us to become the true persons we are called to become.

Grace refers to the graciousness of God, who supports and maintains us in this journey. Grace is the overflowing, everpresent favor of God. It refers to the initiative of God to fashion what we are asked to become. Grace refers to that power and presence, that movement and rhythm and timing of the Spirit of God that maintains and prompts us to move forward.

Sometimes grace flows into us directly through prayer, meditation, scripture, sacraments, or ritual. Sometimes grace comes indirectly through people who cross our paths, events that take place, or circumstances that come together, allowing us to make the changes we need to make, that we had not anticipated.

We often experience grace at a feeling level when we are filled with peace and joy and freedom; at a thinking level through the emergence of new ideas, inspiration, and insights; at an intuitive level when we are able—through inner knowing—to grasp and understand reality. For example, sometimes I receive a telephone call "out of the blue" that offers me an opportunity. Sometimes I meet the right person with the right message. Sometimes I am directed to the right place and I discover a solution.

I see our human journey as one of unfoldment. As we move, for example, new insights, talents, awareness, discipline, and freedom open within us. In the human experience, what is this process of unfoldment? It includes our development from human being to human person to spirit person.

Most of us have no problem with the concept of personhood. We know and we see how we develop intellectually, physically, emotionally, socially, sexually, morally, and ethically through our years from infancy through adulthood. We have ample evidence of this personally and socially.

We also recognize how we learn to make choices and value the gift and responsibility of choice, how we deepen our perception and grasp reality. Additionally we understand how we learn to give and receive love, recognize our value, affirm and protect our dignity, overcome resistance, and develop our creativity.

We catch a glimpse of our spirit at work, here and there, and of our call to become co-creators with God. We experience the awakening of our intuition. We learn to listen for the still small "voice," and we learn to be discerning.

Sometimes, however, the human ego can be an obstacle in this unfoldment. Sometimes our ego blocks the movement of the Spirit within us, and among us, because, to participate in that realm, we are not asked to exercise control, but to surrender, to cooperate, to be open, to respond to a higher wisdom, a greater, more embracing love. We are asked to trust the invisible, the unseen, the altogether holy, the altogether lovely.

The human ego says, "I can make things happen my way. I know what is needed. I know what should work. I will control circumstances. I will decide and execute my decisions. I am powerful."

This line of reasoning and expectation serves us

well in basic earthly life, but our purpose for being human is not only ego development. That, in fact, is a superficial outer part of us. There is a much more real, a much deeper level of self that needs to be recognized and developed. Crisis in life, disappointment, death, the call of God on our life, will often "crack" the human ego shell. This is a way to remove biases, limitations, mistaken beliefs, ideas, feelings, and prejudices from our sense of self. When this happens we can realize more fully the essential aspects of our self. Deeper powers, greater gifts, and talents are then allowed to come through. Often a new courage, faith, wisdom, and awareness unfold in our living and embrace of reality.

We see a similar analysis when we try to contemplate God's eternal design for ourselves. For example, in the unborn child living in the womb, we see the development of a whole system. We know that he can hear music but does not know that he will play an instrument or compose a sonata someday. We know that he hears speech but does not know that he will speak and make eloquent speeches someday.

So much of this can be applied also to ourselves as earthly beings and eternal beings. So much of what is in process or sensed is not yet realized or expressed in our lives here on Earth. So many of our spiritual faculties and powers that are in embryonic stages here unfold more completely eternally: consciousness, creativity, spiritual vision, faith, love, dominion, imagination, and will, to name but a few.

I am reminded of a story written by Norman Vincent Peale that appeared many years ago in *Guideposts* magazine about Cecil B. DeMille, the famous motion picture producer.

DeMille was in a canoe on a lake in Maine thinking out a problem. When the canoe came to rest in a shallow area DeMille noticed a number of water beetles below the surface. One of them crawled up the side of the canoe and died.

He returned to his reflection process trying to come to some solution to his problem. After some grappling with this he turned his attention again to the beetle. As he did, he witnessed its transformation. The shell of the beetle had become dry and brittle due to the penetrating rays of the sun. Before his eyes, the shell split open, "and from there it slowly emerged a dragonfly, which finally took to the air, its scintillating colors flashing in the sunlight."

It was now freer than it had been and more empowered to move in ways and with breadth and speed impossible before in its water beetle state. Its former companions still living below could not comprehend this glorious freedom and new airborne life. They were still bound by their earthly existence and function.

As time passed, DeMille shared this experience with others, along with some of his reflections. "Would the great creator of the universe," he asked, "do that for a water beetle and not for a human being?"[1]

Cecil DeMille didn't think so. Norman Vincent Peale didn't think so either. I know it's not so, from my many experiences with those who have died and lived on in the next world.

How do we as human persons living here on Earth catch a glimpse of and come to sense this new life and recognize the unfolding capacities of our spirit friends?

Recently as I was taking my daily four-mile walk, I was deeply in prayer for a time, absorbing, enjoying, and thanking God for the quiet and beauty surrounding me. I felt a sweet clarity and freedom fill my spirit and an opening take place in my consciousness. Then I received a message from my deceased colleague and treasured friend, Bill Downey. It seemed to float through my spirit. "In this world," he said, "we wear our thoughts the way humans wear their clothes on Earth. When you look around, people are dressed in outfits easily seen and able to be identified. We do the same with our thoughts."

I continued to walk and reflect and sing softly. I have known for some time that those at the higher levels, on occasion in my life, have been able to read, anticipate, and respond to my thoughts because of their greater knowledge, expanded awareness, and vision. I had earlier experienced this, especially with Rudolph Morris, Doris Myhre, and my father.

It surely makes more sense to me, now, knowing that the world of those living on the next levels of consciousness thrives on thought communication, thought forms, and thought evolution. It is clearer to me now that they participate more skillfully and consciously in the mind and heart of God-Christ. It is clearer to me that they learn how to direct that energy experience and learn how to live more creatively, reflecting more of spiritual truth and love and joy and healing.

It is very clear to me that just as we here on Earth through time must become aware of ourselves as physical beings with mental faculties and use and develop our bodies and minds positively and productively, our departed loved ones must also learn of themselves as spirit persons. Those who die and leave their Earth home must learn and know and accept themselves as spirits. They must develop more fully and actively as spirit persons in light of God's call and purpose for them in the heavenly realms. As this unfolds they more fully enjoy the delights of God and experience spiritual fulfillment, spiritual harmony, and greater intimacy with God and other spirit persons like them.

How often do we here on Earth struggle with, and fall victim to, negative thinking? How valuable is it to nurture and train positive thinking and possibility thinking for ourselves and others? How worthy is it for each of us to follow the biblical prescription: "Finally, brethren, whatever things are true, whatever things are noble, whatever things are just, whatever things are pure, whatever things are lovely, whatever things are of good report, if there is any virtue and if there is anything praiseworthy—meditate on these." (Phil. 4:8).

I have struggled some time in my own life with confusion and this challenge of cultivating right thinking and remaining centered in Christ. Sometimes distractions would come and initially appear attractive and harmless enough as I entertained them. Soon enough I would find myself unfocused, diminished, fixated, or wasting time and energy yearning for God's direction again, yearning for God's sweet peace and clarity, yearning to rest in the love and light of the Divine Spirit once more.

In James Allen's classic *As a Man Thinketh,* which has been transcribed for women under the title *As a Woman Thinketh* by Dorothy J. Hulst, we read: "Keep your hand firmly upon the balm of thought. In the back of your soul reclines the commanding Master. He does not sleep: wake Him."[2] She continues, reminding us of the incomparable worth and strength of self-control in every individual's life. True peace and power come to each of us when we learn to master our thoughts.

Let us return to ego growth and soul growth here in human life. How do we distinguish between them? When I am engaged in ego growth I seek to maintain my boundaries. I know what my rights and responsibilities are and what yours are. I seek to honor and protect my feelings so I do not invite injury or tolerate being discounted. I seek to defend myself under attack, to make and execute right decisions, to achieve competence in my work and relationships, to gain recognition, to stand on principles.

On Earth we must value ego growth. In this culture, however, we often value ego supremacy. Sometimes we do this to such a degree that we breed arrogance and human invincibility.

When I am engaged in soul growth, I seek to understand who I am in light of my creator, who I am

as a child of God, who I am eternally. I seek to develop
faith in God, to taste and see the Divine. I seek to grow
in fortitude, increase in wisdom, develop creativity. I
seek to practice humility, patience, perseverance,
compassion, and gratitude. I seek to value and honor
integrity and courage and love in human life and
human relationships. I seek to know and surrender to
the will of God.

In what ways do we learn these qualities—qualities
which open us to the Spirit of God? How do we learn
to surrender to and cooperate with the ways and laws
of God in our homes, relationships, families, work,
communities, and governments?

There is often a stark contrast in these levels of
growth. For example, an article entitled "In the Valley
of the Shadow" by the late Carl Sagan appeared in
Parade magazine, March 10, 1996.

In it Sagan revealed a conclusion about the afterlife
that is in sharp contrast to my own. On at least four
occasions in his life, Dr. Sagan intimately confronted
the face of death. Each time he was spared. However,
he recognized clearly that at some time and in some
way death would claim him.

These four confrontations proved to be meaningful
learning experiences for him. Through them he deepened his faith and appreciation of the sweet intrinsic

value of beauty, love, friendship, and family in human life. Because of these gifts, Dr. Sagan goes on to admit that he would like to believe he would continue to live after his death and have some part of his consciousness continue. But he recognizes that such desires are in the nature of wishful thinking—even though belief in the afterlife characterizes many cultural traditions throughout time.[3]

How sad, in my judgment, this conclusion is. And how wrong. I contrast this now with a segment from a meditation I wrote in 1991 for my Church Lenten Journal, "Doors That Keep Opening." I concluded that piece with the following quotation from Bob and Elizabeth Dole's book, *The Doles: Unlimited Partners:*

> I am reminded that what we do on our own matters little—what counts is what God chooses to do through us. Life is more than a few years spent on self-indulgence or career advancement. It's a privilege, a responsibility and a stewardship to be met according to His calling."[4]

I say, "Deo Gratias, Deo Gratias."

Biblically, I am drawn to Jeremiah 18:1-7: "... says the Lord. Look, as the clay is in the potter's hand, so are you in my hand."

I am reminded, when I look closely at life, how many times the Lord has fashioned and refashioned me. As I contemplate this I sense a prayer being formed and rising from deep within me:

> Dearest God, keep me open to your artistry in my being
> and becoming. Hold me in your infinite patience as I
> learn to recognize and respond to your wisdom and
> delight.

One of my most nourishing Christian hymns is
"Spirit of the Living God." I often find myself spontaneously singing this. I intend to be doing so throughout eternity, as I rise higher and higher in love and
thought, wider in Divine consciousness, deeper in
relationship with God and others like me and more
active in the advancing mission and call God has on
my life.

> Spirit of the Living God, fall afresh on me.
> Spirit of the Living God, fall afresh on me.
> Melt me, mold me, fill me, use me.
> Spirit of the Living God, fall afresh on me.

In my monthly seminar, "Healing and Growing
Through Grief," which I offer for the public at Wisconsin Memorial Park, I tell my dear participants that
God's energy is moving in our lives at all times, and I
ask these questions: Do we recognize that? Do we
respond to that energy? And do we integrate that
energy in our lives?

These are three different questions. Distractions
and temptations are abundant. The forces of darkness

and evil seek to weaken us, dissipate our energies, oppress us, cause us to compromise and feed on defeat.

I would ask you to ask yourself now, how do you center into the energy of God each day? It's a crucial question, and it requires a response from you, followed by a decision to honor your answer.

The God of intelligence, creativity, and love is intimately fashioning who and what we become. The Bible speaks of us as children of God made in the image and likeness of God.

I see eternity as the continuing unfoldment and completion of that identity, the continuing development and expression of that relationship, and the continuing development and expression of spiritual consciousness. The eternal journey is a progressive unfoldment of our individual spiritual self in relationship to the God of our being. We share this continuing life with others engaged in God's mission and others who share similar levels of consciousness.

It's a progressive unfoldment. It does not happen all at once or at any one point. How do you unfold as spirit? How do you manifest as spirit? How do you know yourself as spirit with powers, talents, mission, and freedom? How did Jesus come to know and manifest Himself as Spirit?

At a higher level, eternity is coming to know the
Mind, the Heart, and the Spirit of God. There are
various sides of this unfoldment. There is the unfoldment of our spiritual personhood and the developing
use of our spiritual energy. There is the unfoldment of
relationship with the Divine. There is the revelation,
discovery, and embrace of the God of creation / salva-
tion / eternity. This God seeks to be known, loved, and
trusted. We are made for intimacy with God, to be in
communion, to be in communication with God, to
know and understand the movements of God. In
doing so we become most authentically who we are.

God cares passionately about us individually and
has a profound personal commitment to each of us.
Biblically, in the Judeo-Christian tradition, we have
evidence of this through our mothers and fathers in
the faith, the prophets, and Jesus Christ. As an individual, when and where have you been inspired and
directed by the Spirit of God? Where have you encountered Christ personally as the healer, felt the comfort of
Mary in the hurts of your life, or perhaps been touched
by an angel thought or guided by an angel presence?
How has this made you more aware spiritually, more
empowered, more committed, more complete?

To speak more now of eternity: In traditional
Judeo-Christian religious teachings, depending on our

tradition, we are taught that when we die, we go to heaven, hell, or purgatory. Many Christian teachings state explicitly or assume that when we die our destiny is determined. When many people consider eternity, if they do, it is usually as a static concept.

I want us to understand that those of us who are ready, when we die, we enter heaven and heaven and heaven. It is an experience of ascending. We find confirmation for this in the writings of saints, mystics, and gifted psychics, and in traditional religious teachings. In Job 22:12, Job asks, "Is God not in the height of heaven?" In St. Paul's writings, he speaks of being taken up into the third heaven.[5] In *The Last Battle,* C.S. Lewis writes that earthly life is the cover and title page of a book. He writes of heaven as the chapters ahead.

In Rose Ann Bradley's illuminating article "A Child's View of Heaven," which appeared in *Marriage and Family Living,* August 1987, we have a wonderful testimony of faith in eternal life. Rose Ann writes to her bereaved sister at the time of the death of her five year old son, Scott. Mrs. Bradley awakens her readers to this remarkable truth:

> Heaven is not a passive gazing at God, listening to choirs of angels, or an eternal vacation at the beach. It is an active, creative place of learning and growing. [6]

I advise my students and clients to meditate on this several times a year. Later, Mrs. Bradley refers to Dr. Peter Kreeft's book, *Everything You Ever Wanted to Know About Heaven,* in which he writes of the Beatific Vision as an experience of exploration "as endless beginnings rather than merely the end." How wondrous that experience will be for each of us; how precious Divine life really is. I, for one, am filled with breathtaking anticipation and confidence in God as I contemplate all that God has yet to offer me eternally. Is this not also true for you?

Now let us return to the unfoldment process. It happens when we are prepared and ready and God calls us forward. We then move on higher and higher. Ascending depends on our perception, response, discernment, and development. Ascending is fashioned by the Spirit of God, by God's Grace offered freely to us throughout eternity, and in our response.

To gain a better understanding of eternity, it is helpful to look at what are called non-ordinary states of consciousness. Ordinary states of consciousness locate us in three dimensional states of being: time, space, and matter. These states can be explained and observed. We prepare people for these. We can antici-pate these, analyze and evaluate these.

When we enter non-ordinary states of consciousness, these boundaries drop or dissolve. We are no longer able to identify experience at those levels. Other levels are to be considered. Who is it that treats the study of this reality? Transpersonal psychologists, Jungian psychologists, gifted psychics, serious mystics, poets, philosophers, and deeply developed religious people. Traditional psychologists usually won't touch it.

To gain a better grasp of non-ordinary states of consciousness, let's turn to what psychologists refer to as peak experiences in life. On a natural level, peak experiences include experiencing simultaneous sexual orgasm, being caught up in the visual artistry of the fall foliage, entering into an orchestral concert—losing yourself in its melody and harmony, and watching figure skaters absorbed in the flow and harmony and elevation of their dance. In peak experiences, our ordinary boundaries seem to dissolve. Participants enter into joy, wonder, unity, freedom, and bliss.

Peak experiences at a supernatural level would include mystical union with God, the anointing of the Holy Spirit, being caught up in contemplative prayer, offering charismatic prayer, and yoga masters' achieving levitation.

Non-ordinary states of consciousness can be induced by fasting, meditation, drumming, sleep deprivation, drugs, contemplative prayer, charismatic prayer, and jogging.

In the book *Intangible Evidence,* Bernard Gittelson writes:

> Evidence of seemingly paranormal goings-on come in from all over—from many different fields, from many different belief systems, and from all corners of the world. . . . What we are learning about paranormal phenomena flies in the face of everything we have been taught about the nature of reality.[7]

Non-ordinary states of consciousness include: Out-of-body experiences (which include near-death experience), deathbed visions, mystic visions, apparitions, materialization, mediumship, reincarnation, and electric communication with the dead. We will look at some of these in the following chapters.

CHAPTER THREE

NEAR-DEATH EXPERIENCES

Before Raymond Moody wrote *Life After Life,* there was no real professional interest in the subject of near-death experience (NDE) and almost no research. Several pioneers emerged with Dr. Moody, for example, Dr. Elisabeth Kübler-Ross, Dr. Kenneth Ring, and Dr. Melvin Morse.

One hundred years ago, our standards related to death and dying were different. In some sense, as a people, we seem to have leaped forward, both at a societal level and at an individual level. To begin with, we are more knowledgeable today about the process and reality of death and dying (and, I would like to suggest, after death.) Dr. Carol Zaleski of Harvard, for example, has written a provocative book, *Otherworld Journeys,* in which she tells us that much of the literature of the Middle Ages is filled with similar accounts.

We may conclude then that only the NDE research is new and not the NDE itself.

Ray Moody in his early research is very careful to tell us that NDEs do not prove that life after death occurs. Moody says: "I don't think science can ever answer that question."[1] In addition, NDE studies in total cannot be replicated. Elisabeth Kübler-Ross, on the other hand, after studying some 20,000 NDEs, diverges and says that because of NDE research we will ultimately understand that death is not the end, but a new beginning. Death is a transition into a higher state of consciousness.

To what do we refer when we talk of NDEs? Essentially, these involve people who, in cases of accident, cardiac arrest, severe injury, near drowning, extreme illness, or attempted suicide, come near death. With clinical death or near death some people who are declared dead are brought back from death and report being alive the entire time.

Polls taken in the last two decades indicate that more than eight million Americans have had near-death experiences.[2] This does not mean all have had a full composite NDE, an experience containing all of the reported characteristics.

Not everyone pronounced clinically dead remembers or reports having such an experience. Though there are wide similarities, no two cases are identical. There are a few critics who believe that some NDE cases reveal influences of the occult world. No doubt this is valid, given the mosaic of personalities and the unique histories of the people involved.

Some criticisms challenge the explanation of the NDE, which you will find in Chapter Seven, "Explanations," of Moody's book *The Light Beyond.* I'm satisfied, given the responses of reputable researchers, that most NDE research and reports are authentic. Some people who report experiences that are unclear or negative realize, in the long run, that these experiences can be transforming for them. When they process through the meaning and obstacles involved, they arrive at new truth, understanding, faith, and freedom.

Moody observes that interviews with those reporting NDEs reveal several similarities, such as:

1. Having an authority declare them dead and officially confirming this to others.
2. Feeling an initial sense of pleasantness, contentment, and tranquillity.
3. Experiencing intense unpleasant sounds and feeling terror or regret at or near death.
4. Feeling as if they were being drawn quickly through a tunnel-like space.
5. Gazing upon one's human body, feeling detached

and removed, aware of oneself as a spirit moving.

6. Being aware of and communicating with other spiritual beings.

7. Perceiving other spiritual beings who are struggling, trapped, or confined in a state of consciousness that limits them, unable or unwilling to detach their energy from the materialistic, sensual, or addictive, and who must work to release these fixations and attachments so they can embrace and absorb more of the life of God.

8. Encountering some degree of Divine light, and experiencing it progressively, from dim to bright. Some Christian people, for example, report seeing Christ, Mary, or an Angel. Some Hindus report encountering the gods Vishnu or Shiva.

9. Undergoing many degrees of life review in accelerated rhythm in the presence of a celestial being, feeling the consequences of one's actions, becoming aware of heightened responsibility.

10. Experiencing penetrating knowledge and deeply comprehending the meaning of universal life.

11. Seeing and participating in visions of the Spirit worlds beyond.

12. Returning to the physical body and to earthly life, initially feeling regret about doing so, and sometimes caught in painful readjustments.[3]

I'd like to explore a few of these characteristics. Let us focus, to start, on number 5, looking down at one's own physical body from a point outside of it and floating in a weightless spiritual body. One of the things this phenomenon tells us is that the boundaries of time and space were broken while the individuals were out of their bodies. Their ability to see, hear, and understand was not dependent on the brain. Consciousness is greater than the brain and takes these individuals where they need to be.

NDEs report that while watching their doctors work on them in the operating room, they could move easily into the waiting room to see their friends and relatives. In *The Light Beyond,* Dr. Moody writes of one such experience involving an elderly woman who was resuscitated. As the surgeon was giving her closed heart massage, his attending nurse was sent to get a vial of medication outside the emergency room.

Because the top of the glass vial needed to be broken off, the nurse should have placed it in protective cloth or paper towel to protect her hand from glass splinters. But to save time, when the nurse returned to the physician she handed him the vial minus its neck. Upon regaining consciousness, the patient looked at the nurse and with great sweetness said, "Honey, I saw what you did in that room, and you're going to cut

yourself doing that." The nurse confessed that because
time was so limited she had broken off the glass neck
with her bare hand. The elderly patient reported that
in the process of her resuscitation on the table, she had
followed the nurse to the other room and been able to
observe exactly what she was doing. This kind of
expanded movement and perceptive observation is
reported by many undergoing emergency surgery.

In *Parting Visions,* Dr. Melvin Morse tells of another
experience of this kind involving a twenty-four-year-
old woman during a traumatic labor. To deliver this
young woman's baby by cesarean section, the doctors
gave her only a spinal anesthetic. No other drugs were
administered.

During the delivery she was drawn out of her body
into a realm of radiant light. While there, surrounded
by an atmosphere of love, she was told she could not
stay and that her baby would not live on Earth. She
was assured her daughter would be loved, nurtured,
and protected. "When the doctors told her that her
baby girl was stillborn and had never taken her first
breath of life, she told them that she already knew and
explained what had happened. She told her doctors
that she had been in a ball of light with her child and
knew God would be taking care of her."[4]

We know when we speak of eternity it is outside

the realm of earthbound time. Time as we know it, clock hours, is a human convention which makes things easier, practical, and more efficient. On Earth it is a necessity. In eternity it is irrelevant.

What major lessons flow from those who have had an NDE? One is that learning doesn't stop when we die. Each of us takes the knowledge and learning we have with us into the next level of consciousness. Another lesson is that love is the most important value in earthly life. In American culture this is an important lesson, indeed, because most often, in earthly life, material accumulation and wealth are promoted as the pinnacle of achievement.

In all my experience with those who have died, these lessons of learning and love are clearly communicated to me over and over again.

In his book *The Journey Home: What Near Death-Experiences and Mysticism Teach Us About the Gift of Life*, Dr. Phillip Berman has written an extensive account of the near-death experience of Dr. George Rodonaia, a man who holds an M.D., a Ph.D. in neuropathology, and a Ph.D. in the psychology of religion.

Dr. Berman tells us that in a keynote address to the United Nations in 1993 on "The Emerging Global Spirituality," Dr. Rodonaia described working as a neuropathologist when living in Russia some twenty years earlier and devoting himself to psychiatric research at the University of Moscow. At that time in his life he was an avowed atheist. In 1976 in Thilisi, Soviet Georgia, he was involved in a head-on automobile accident and left three days in a morgue. He did not "return to life" until a doctor began to make an incision as part of an autopsy.

Dr. Rodonaia reported that at the point of his accidental death, he entered deep darkness, then bright light. He was aware he was still alive—alive but living in another dimension. This was shocking to him. As quoted by Dr. Berman, Dr. Rodonaia says of his experience, "I saw the universal form of life and nature laid out before my eyes. It was clear to me that I didn't need my body any more, it was actually a limitation."[5] He experienced the greatest sense of peace, joy, unity, and wholeness while he was in the light.

It was when they were performing an autopsy on him that he felt as though he had been pushed back into his physical body. The pain of the knife jolted him, and he opened his eyes. He remained hospitalized for nine months and kept on a respirator.

Following this spiritually transforming experience, when he regained his health he returned to the University of Georgia to earn a Ph.D. in the psychology of religion. He continued to pursue his religious development and was ordained a priest in the Eastern Orthodox Church. In 1989 he and his family came to the United States. Dr. Rodonaia then served as an associate pastor at the First United Methodist Church in Nederland, Texas, for two years. Currently, Pastor Rodonaia is Director of the La Mar University Wesley Foundation in Belmont, Texas, and also teaches comparative religion, philosophy of religion, and psychology of religion at the university.

God is, Dr. Rodonaia believes, beyond our ability to comprehend totally and the universe is a marvelous mystery. "To serve God's creations with a warm and loving hand of generosity and compassion—that is the only meaningful existence."[6]

Dr. Rodonaia realizes that in spite of his own profound NDE, he has no absolute answers or exclusive claim on Truth. He believes that it is only when each person dies and makes his own transition that he will come into union with the Divine and comprehend eternal truth and reality.

Researchers of near-death experiences have collected data from people cross-culturally and cross-generationally, and from every religious tradition including from those who call themselves atheists or agnostics. The data seem to suggest that this experience changes the perspective of a person and the meaning he or she assigns to life.

I want now to conclude this chapter with a profoundly personal and transforming experience of my
own which occurred Wednesday evening, November
10, 1993.

I must begin by putting this within its proper
context. For most of my adult life, at least for the last
twenty-five years, one of my main spiritual interests as
an educator has been spiritual healing. Though I did
not focus there exclusively, it was central to my identity and journey. I studied all the traditional Christian
approaches, the Charismatic approach, along with the
metaphysical approaches: Christian Science, Religious
Science, and Unity.

I taught college classes and community seminars in
Wellness and Holistic Heath, and I lectured around the
country on this subject and on Dr. Bernie Siegel's book
Love, Medicine and Miracles.

In my own lifetime I had many spiritual healings:
internal bleeding, migraine headaches, allergy, and a
lower back problem, to name a few. I took no medication for fifteen years. Because of my healings I was
able to bypass any surgery or treatment.

In early April 1993 I had a critical health challenge
which I was unable to treat spiritually as I had the
other challenges in the past. I did have surgery and I

did cooperate with my physicians and all follow-up treatment.

Initially, for me, succumbing to surgery and treatment was a major failing, and I felt numb and disoriented spiritually. It put me at a very different place with God in my life. In addition I really didn't know what God was asking of me, and I didn't know how to make sense of it all. So I started out on a different path, and more opened before me, but I was still very numb. I tried to intensify my prayer life. I still felt numb.

In early summer, Mary, the mother of Jesus, reached out to me. Whenever I came into her presence, unbelievable pain would rise to the surface and pour forth—pain I did not know I had. Over a span of time, healing insights flowed through me. I tasted often of the loveliness of Mary and felt her deep comfort, and I came to know her wisdom.

Yet I did not know what God was asking of me or where I was going with all of this. I was concentrating on putting everything in my life in order and completing it so that I could move on.

I was working at that time as a grief counselor at a local funeral home and conducting four evening grief groups each week. On Wednesday evening I shared an audio tape, "The Healing Journey," with my group. The tape recording took us into a meditation/visualization exercise that was very effective.

The narrator invited us to treat illness/disease as an unwanted temporary intruder and to dissolve, distract, and eliminate it in various ways. When we concluded, four of my group members asked me to order the tape for them. I agreed and sent my group home. I decided that I needed to listen to the tape a second time as well.

I arrived home at 9:45 P.M. and took my nightly bath. My usual ritual was to fill the bathtub to the very top and spend an hour there reading. I did not answer phone calls during that time. However, this night I decided that rather than reading I would listen to the tape again. I felt it had depth and substance. I knew I wouldn't have time to do so later in the week. It was a thirty-minute tape.

I placed my cassette tape recorder on the corner of the bathtub and proceeded to plug it in around the mirror over the sink. I turned the lights off, turned the recorder on, and submerged myself in the water.

Roughly twenty minutes passed and I thought, "This water is getting cool. I should add more hot water," but I did not do so. Just then the tape recorder fell into the tub, sending electric currents through the water. My right foot banged against the side of the tub again and again. The room was totally dark; I could see nothing. When I realized what was happening, I screamed "Help, help!" With that I started to go under, swallowing water. I knew, then, it was all over and silently said, "Lord, have mercy." I went under. I don't know how long I was under but I felt the tiniest piece of energy pick me up out of the water and a heavier energy carry me over and deposit me on the floor on my knees. There I was on my hands and knees on the floor, my shower cap off and my hair dripping wet. Slowly I became aware of what had happened. At the same time a stillness surrounded me, as if I was being focused to pay attention. There was a very peaceful, dark, powerful presence behind me to my right, or within me to my right. Once I focused and became aware, I wondered if I could still use my mind and body. I tried to count numbers, spell words, and move my fingers. (I have long been terrified of suffering a stroke as my father had.) I could do all of that. Then I tried to move and sit on the toilet seat lid. I did so and flipped on the light. I was still aware that this peaceful, loving, dark powerful presence was with me. I looked at my leg. It was fine, but my toes on my right foot had cuts on them. I looked over at the bathtub. The cassette recorder was in it—the plastic piece was slightly broken off, and the tape was floating in the water, as well as the entire cord.

I wrapped my body and head in towels and walked into my bedroom. As I faced the side of my bed, I reached for my robe lying on the bed. As I did, thick ovals of energy moving from head to toe broke out in front of me, on my right side. Out of my mouth came the words, "God wants you alive and alive for a reason." I put my robe on, walked to get an ice pack for my foot, and went into the living room. As I sat down I thought, "I need someone to pray with me." I glanced over at the clock—11:20 P.M. So I dismissed that idea, and after nursing my foot, I went to bed.

Once in bed, I wanted to read my bible. However, to do so I would have to get out of bed again and take it from my bookcase. However, just that morning I had put on my nightstand a small red booklet from the Robert Schuller Ministries, *Positive Encouragement For You: 365 Promises of Hope From the Heart of God.* I opened it at random and read out loud: DO YOUR BEST AND LEAVE THE REST TO ME. This was followed by scriptural quotations, which I read silently and reflectively.

Do not neglect the gift that is in you . . .
. . . that your progress may be evident to all
(1 Tim. 4:14, 15)
Be strong and do not let your hands be weak, for your work shall be rewarded.
(2 Chron. 15:7)
Let your light so shine that others may see your

good works and glorify your Father in heaven

(Matt. 5:16)

For we are His workmanship, created in Christ
Jesus for good works.

(Eph. 2:10)

Whoever gives a little one a cup of cold water,
shall by no means lose their reward.

(Matt. 10:42)

For it is God who works in you both to will and
to do for his good pleasure.

(Phil. 2:13)

Be confident of this very thing, that He who has
begun a good work in you will complete it.

(Phil. 1:6)

I put the book down after a few minutes of reflection. I thought, "Perhaps it would be a good thing
tonight to sleep with the light on." Just then, a voice as
audible as my own said, "Why, Jacqui, are you afraid?"
I said, "No, I'm not afraid anymore," and with that I
turned the light off. The presence passed through me
on the right side and moved on. I slept through the
night.

When I awoke the next morning, I recalled everything. I recited some of the scriptural passages,
counted numbers, spelled words, and moved my arms
and legs. I was fine. When I got out of bed my foot was
black and blue, but it didn't hurt. All morning I went

about the house very quietly and very slowly, trying to understand it all. I was filled with the most incredible love and peace I have ever known. It just kept rising up in me and flowing out—rising up and flowing out. By noontime, I decided I needed to tell someone about this, so I called my internist. He is intelligent and spiritually developed, and we have had long talks together through the years. I talked with his nurse, Carolyn, and said that I had an accident in the bathtub and I needed to talk with Dr. Auger. I told her that I didn't need him to attend to me but I needed him for security purposes.

Five minutes later he phoned and asked what happened. I told him the story. He listened intensely and then asked me if my leg was burned or lacerated in any way. I said, "No." He then asked how deep the cuts were. I said, "Not deep at all. The deepest is on my little toe and I treated it with Neosporin and there is not a problem."

I said, "I want to know if there will be any long-term repercussions." (He knew I feared a stroke.) Dr. Auger replied, "Long-term repercussions? Jacqui, you were electrocuted in that bathtub last night and the Lord delivered you. You should be grateful." "Whoa," I said, "I'm grateful, I'm profoundly grateful. I just did not want to come to you one month from now with symptoms and have you ask why I didn't report it when it happened." He said he was glad I called, and if I would like to come in he would examine me. "I'm fine," I said. "I've never been so fine." Just before ending our conversation, Dr. Auger added, "You know, Jacqui, this is a very profound happening and you need to do something more with it." He was indeed right.

I prayed the scriptures. Slowly and selectively I shared my story with one or two others and occasionally with a small group or two. Over time, I came to realize that God was also trying to tell me what I had to learn from my deliverance. The Lord wanted me, in fact, to take my mind off dying and put it back on His power in my life. I was to invest again in healing and the work he was calling me to. I understood this more clearly . . . and each day forward I was able to follow more closely. I also learned not to ever take a tape recorder into the bathroom!!

During the next six months I was given the message that I needed to be speaking about Angels. Within that year, I designed a mini-seminar for church and then a fully developed seminar on "All About Angels" for Wisconsin Memorial Park. It opened up wide vistas of understanding and experience for me within the celestial spheres.

CHAPTER FOUR

OUR SECOND BODY

I want to turn our attention now to our "second body"—the body that is reported to exist by persons having a near-death experience when physicians report there are neither measurable brain activity nor any physical signs of life whatsoever.

Ray Moody says that it has shape, form, and substance. Dr. Kübler-Ross, after working with hundreds of resuscitated patients, refers to this as a temporary, ethereal body in which we experience completeness, restoration, and the absence of pain and limitation. For example, blind persons are able to see, deaf persons are able to hear and talk, paralyzed persons are able to move and dance.

Skeptics, upon learning of these phenomena, say they are a projection of wishful thinking on the part of the patients in order to relieve their suffering. Dr. Kübler-Ross finds it easy to evaluate whether or not the phenomena are a projection of wishful thinking. She writes in *On Life After Death* that half the cases have been sudden unexpected accidents or near-death experiences in which the subjects were unable to foresee what was going to hit them. She describes the case of a hit-and-run victim whose legs were amputated.

She writes: "When the patient was out of his physical body, he saw his amputated legs on a highway, yet he was fully aware of having both of his legs on his eternal, perfect and whole body. We cannot assume that he had previous knowledge of the loss of his legs and would therefore project in his own wishful thinking that he would be able to walk again."

Kübler-Ross says, however, there is a simpler way to rule out the projection of wishful thinking, and that is to study blind people who do not have light perception. She writes:

> We asked them to share with us what it was like when they had this near-death experience. If it was just wish fulfillment, these blind people would not be able to share with us the color of a sweater, the design of a tie, or many details of shape, colors, designs of people's clothing. We have questioned several totally blind people and they were not only able to tell us who came into the room first and who worked on the resuscitation, but they were able to give minute details of the attire and the clothing of all

the people present, something a totally blind person would never be able to do. [1]

St. Paul (1 Cor. 15:44), speaking of the glorious body—the resurrected body—says, "It is sown a natural body, it is raised a spiritual body."

As spirit persons, at various levels in eternity, we are elevated to and develop powers and qualities so much greater than we had on Earth. To begin with, when we leave a physical material plane, we enter a more spiritual atmosphere free of disease, poverty, immobility, retardation, and ignorance. We have and use different levels of giftedness and skills in eternity. Changes accompany our transition.

For example, we have more freedom and agility. We have the ability to move instantaneously. We have the ability to pass through solid objects. We have the ability to communicate telepathically.

Christian scripture tells us that these changes are beyond our total comprehension now (1 John 3:2). But we do get hints and revelations. We do get partial explanations and we do have experiences with those who have gone ahead of us.

Jesus Himself gave Peter, John, and James a taste of this on the Mount of Transfiguration with two of God's chosen vessels, Jewish holy men, Moses and Elijah.

I want to refer to my experience with many spirit

persons who have died and live in the next world. What have I learned from these spirit persons of the spiritual body?

When we pass over we retain our own personalities. There is a distinct and unique energy within and with each spirit person. For example, the energy and the spirit of my brother, Michael, is easily distinguished from the energy and spirit of my father. We retain our talents and develop further.

In Spirit we are able to think, see, move, feel, create, pray, praise, and serve. We are able to learn, love, know, teach, heal, and choose.

When we are born and arrive here to participate on planet Earth, we must learn that we have a physical body, that we are physical beings, and that we have to learn how to use our physical bodies. When we die and enter the next world, we change. We must learn that we are spirit persons, that we have a spiritual body, and that we need to learn how to participate, move, and develop as spirits.

Emmanuel Swedenborg, an influential scientist, mystic, philosopher, and theologian of the seventeenth century, had a number of dreams that moved him profoundly. In a subsequent vision God made known to him further divine revelations through his writings. He wrote extensively about these experiences.

Swedenborg believed deeply in man's spirit and in the afterlife. He claimed that man's spirit, which is his mind in his body, is in its entire form a man. "Man after death is just as much as he was in the world, with this difference only, that he cast off the coverings that formed his body in the world."[2]

To understand this more clearly, permit me now to go directly to the life of Jesus of Nazareth, the Risen Christ. For those of you reading this who share this faith tradition or for those of you who have a personal relationship with and experience of Christ, this will be more readily understood and felt. Those of you who come to Christ metaphysically likewise will appreciate the meaning of the Truth of Christ. For those of you who don't, I offer the example of Jesus Christ as a model to you of what can take place following death.

What do we see in the Gospels after the death of Jesus? He returns to those He loved, trained, and taught. His body is recognizable to them. He instructs them "to touch but not cling." He speaks, He breaks bread (a symbol of great significance to them), He enters rooms without knocking. He gives direction. One of the most wonderful things about Jesus, I feel, is His great continuity. He returns, not as a cloud. He returns as Himself, at least in some encounters. In other encounters, He appears at first somewhat disguised (as a gardener, as a stranger), but then He is recognizable to His followers by the tone of His voice or His behavior.

Jesus foretells the future. He gives emotional support and encouragement. He blesses and provides clarity. "Their eyes were opened and they knew Him." (Luke 24:31) He gives instruction . . . "Cast the net on the right side of the boat . . ." (John 21:6) He reads minds and thoughts. He reassures them. "Peace to you." (John 20:21) He speaks of Ascension. "Do not cling to me, for I have not yet ascended to my Father." (John 20:17)

Jesus offers us a wonderful model to try to understand what's happening today as people die and move on and communicate with others at various levels. It helps Christians understand our own continuing relationship and experience of Christ in our lives.

Allow me to share with you an encounter I had with Jesus about two years ago. It was a Monday morning. I had stopped by church to drop off the three meditations I wrote for our Lenten Journal. Before leaving, I stopped in the sanctuary. I sat alone gazing at the altar and the large cross above the altar—struggling in meditation and dialogue for a few minutes with the Lord about some of what seemed unending midlife issues. It seemed to me that I needed to give more attention in myself to a deeper humility and obedience. I was trying to focus on the humility and obedience Jesus demonstrated in His own death. Somehow, I was distracted for a moment to the far left side of the sanctuary and felt the presence of the Lord. As I did, He started to walk slowly away from me and said to me, "But, Jacqui—I walked out of my tomb and never went back."

I sat, awed, reflecting on what had just happened. Where I thought I needed to concentrate my time and energy was not where I needed to be. Clear insights rose rapidly in me. Now was the time I needed to embrace more actively His risen life within me and greet my future. I needed to remove the blockages and barriers of my past experiences. My stone of excuses, reluctance, perfectionism, and regression needed to be rolled away. I needed to come out of my tomb, activate my faith, increase my trust, and demonstrate greater courage. I needed to follow His lead and example more confidently . . . one step at a time. I was grateful, once again, for His competent care and clear knowledge and understanding of me. I left the sanctuary that morning and committed myself to one project that had been stalled for eight months. That evening, I initiated a community program that I had suspected would have little if any merit. It was a complete success.

I want to share the next two experiences of friends who died and moved on. One story occurred about six years ago. I had been passed over for the extension of a teaching contract and was feeling violated by the lack of integrity on the part of an administrator. In addition, I was saddened by the death of a colleague of mine about three weeks earlier, and I was feeling the pain of a back ailment. Quite discouraged and out of sorts, one June evening about 9:00 P.M. I was walking in our cul-de-sac trying to get the exercise I knew would be helpful. I had been at this for about fifteen minutes, lost in my thoughts, when I turned to my right and saw the spirit of Rudolph moving with me. He appeared to be walking in the customary way he had twenty five years earlier . . . with his hands behind his back. I said to him, "I know you are with me and I know you don't want me to feel so discouraged and alone." He didn't respond at first and then he said to me . . . "Do you know what God has in mind for you? Have you forgotten your gifts and talents?" Immediately, a quiet peace settled on me and Rudolph was gone. His visit offered me reassurance and brought me back to where I needed to be.

About two months ago, I was driving my car with two young boys, ages eight and ten, as my passengers. We were all in conversation when I heard a strange

and strong vibration. I didn't know where it was
coming from. I asked the boys to listen for a moment
with me, but it seemed to disappear. We dismissed it.
Two days later, about the dinner hour, I stopped for
groceries before going home. With my grocery bag
intact, I went around to the passenger side of my car to
put it on the seat. Just as I was closing my door I
sensed the spirit of Bill Downey behind me to my
right. As I turned slightly, he directed my focus to the
rear of my car and said, "Look." As I looked down I
saw a crack in the muffler. Very slowly he said, "You
need to have that checked," and left. I took my car to
my regular service station and left it. About an hour
later, Mike, the owner, phoned me. He told me the
entire exhaust system from front to back was gone and
that I needed a new water pump as well as a catalytic
converter. The damaged converter was capable of
leaking carbon monoxide into the car. My car was
repaired and a wave of gentle gratitude floated
through me.

As we study all of the spiritual traditions, it becomes clear that they all give some account of after-
death appearances and communication.

In her most compelling book, *Messengers: After-Death
Appearances of Saints and Mystics,* Patricia Treece reports
the following accounts:

The Hindu Spiritual Master Sri Yukteswar paid an after-death visit to his spiritual son, Paramahansa Yogananda. The Holy Yogananda asked, "But is it you, Master, the same lion of God? Are you wearing a body like the one I buried . . .?" His mentor assured him that this was a created body "made from cosmic atoms" exactly like but not actually the body Yogananda had buried.[3]

Next, Treece quotes from the book *9½ Mystics* by Rabbi Herbert Weiner of Temple Sharey Tefilo-Israel in South Orange, New Jersey, who writes that he studied with a kabbalist by the name of Setzer from New York. Though Setzer was an expert in Jewish mysticism, he defined himself as a "rationalist." Nonetheless, the very true quality of his experience caused him to believe that it was real.

I had two sisters. One of them . . . became seriously ill. One day I was sitting alone in my room and suddenly . . . I am a rationalist, but still, it happened . . . I saw something dressed in black and it was my sister. She came close to me and kissed me, then suddenly dropped away. Then I heard a voice close by, whispering clearly in my ear, "Your sister died, your sister died."[4]

Rabbi Weiner continues the story, describing how Setzer heard beautiful music all the next day so clearly that he was convinced it came from a radio—one his neighbors must have heard playing. To his surprise he learned his neighbors had not heard the music. Then he received a telegram informing him of his sister's death. Weiner reports that Setzer said: "I figured out the time and hour, and it was the exact moment when I heard the whispering."[5]

CHAPTER FIVE

LIFE REVIEW

People from all walks of life and various spiritual traditions have reported their near-death experiences. With these testimonies has developed a more sincere and serious consideration of the life review process. To support this process I refer to an article written by David Lorrimer, Director of the Scientific and Medical Network in England, entitled "Near Death Experiences and Ethical Transformation," which appeared in *Noetic Science Review,* Winter 1994. Dr. Lorrimer writes that the life review, which is often reported as part of the near-death experience:

> . . . characteristically involves "empathetic resonance" which I define as our capacity to experience another person's thoughts and feelings directly. It puts the subject in touch with the interrelatedness and inter-penetration of all things. When what you've given comes back to you exactly in measure. The first step is to be able to forgive yourself, and then start to forgive others.[1]

To exemplify this process, Dr. Lorrimer points to a
prisoner incarcerated for a multitude of felonies.
Apparently, to make prison life somewhat easier for
himself, he ate some soap, hoping to be transferred
and receive care. Physically, acute internal pain re-
sulted. Mental terror and emotional anguish accompa-
nied the pain. This apparently triggered his life review
process, whereby pictures appeared before him. These
included all those whom he had deliberately injured as
well as those who suffered as a result of those inten-
tional injuries. As a consequence, he felt within himself
every pain and hurt he had caused them. Their injustices and suffering became his very own.

Historically, the greatest spiritual masters have
taught that in some way all of our deeds and thoughts
and feelings are recorded at some level. Is this not the
profound meaning of the near-death life review?

Ray Moody offers another story in his book, *The
Light Beyond,* in which we have another testimony of an
NDE from a twenty-three-year-old graduate student in
sociology. This occurred shortly after she finished her
graduate education.

This young woman realized through her experience how liberating it is to accept personal responsibility for everything in one's life. In her life review she
faced directly her failures and successes, her insights

and her blind spots, and felt the consequences of them. As she did she realized each held a valuable lesson for her, and she was determined to learn what that lesson was, so as not to perpetuate emotional pain for herself or for others.

When she was in her life review, reports Moody, absolute honesty was asked of her. "I was the very people that I hurt, and I was the very people that I helped to feel good." This experience helped her to think through many beliefs in her life and redirect the way she lived her daily life.

Martin Buber in his *Tales of the Hasidim* writes that the rabbi of Ger once said: "Why is man afraid of dying? For does he not go to his father! What man fears is the moment he will survey from the other world everything he has experienced on this earth."[2]

Ordinarily, what does this experience of a life review do for NDEs, as well as for those of us who are interested and able to learn vicariously? It helps them to see the importance of their choices. It helps them to develop new ethical and moral principles and live accordingly. It helps them take advantage of opportunities that life presents to them for full human growth and development.

For some people, the life review occurs here on Earth, at their death scene, in their hospital room or when they are diagnosed with a terminal illness. Many dedicated hospice workers attest to this life review being done by their patients.

While I was a graduate student at Marquette University, I sat at the deathbed of Rudolph Morris, who was heavily engaged in life review, though I did not recognize it as such at that time. Sometimes Rudolph did this in Hebrew, sometimes in English. Dr. Morris was a Jew who converted to Catholicism following his holocaust experience.

Rudolph, in revisiting some of his life experiences, would ask, "Have I been helpful enough? Have I trusted God enough and served Him faithfully in these years? Have I been able to ask for forgiveness and accept mercy? Have I brought joy to those I love?"

There are many ways of helping our life review process on this side of life. Traditional religions encourage us to seek answers to questions such as these. Who am I in relation to God? Where am I in relation to God as I understand God? Do I recognize Divine activity? Do I recognize demonic activity? How do I respond? How am I accountable? Where is the place of prayer and meditation, confession, death preparation, atonement, and forgiveness for me? How do I celebrate life? Where is the place of joy in my life?

Forgiveness work must be a priority in human life.

Likewise overcoming fear in life is equally important. Fear can paralyze us in so many direct and subtle ways. Fear can arrest our development. Fear limits movement, preventing us from taking the next step and from moving toward new beginnings. Fear can blind us from asking relevant questions and seeing the pathological. Fear is a hindrance to love. Strictly speaking, though, fear in itself has no power except the power we surrender to it through our thoughts.

In the Old and New Testaments, the words "Fear not" appear seventy-nine times.[3] We encounter fear often in our human lives. Each time we do, it comes to challenge us to develop a greater sense of mastery in life. It is a call to develop greater faith and to exercise wider courage. It is a summons for us to foster positive thinking, feeling and action to whatever degree and in whatever manner possible. We overcome fear as we learn more about the Divine and trust our relationship with God in the here and now and in the life that follows. "I know nothing of death," Martin Buber says, "I know that God is eternal and I know this, too, that he is my God. Whether what we call time remains to us beyond our death becomes quite unimportant to us next to this knowing, that we are God's who is not immortal, but eternal."[4]

Fear has been successful in keeping us locked in

denial and secrecy oftentimes in matters of death, dying and the afterlife. We see in many quarters of the world today positive efforts being made to break through ignorance, passivity, and avoidance in these areas that are the result of many named and unnamed fears. From many quarters, we are trying to help people recognize the value and the process of forgiveness, forgiveness of self, and forgiveness of others. Why is this? Because forgiveness helps us to empty ourselves of bitterness, fear, resentment, hurt, and suffering. Forgiveness allows us to be more receptive to the light and the grace of God. Forgiveness brings clarity and understanding with it. Forgiveness frees us. Often, it seems to me, we become very glib about forgiveness. We merely parrot the word or phrases.

Forgiveness work is just that—work. We must understand and accept how we were wounded, denied, violated, and discounted. We must recognize how deep the hurt was, how serious the betrayal was. We must move back and empty ourselves of that pain and anger. We must come to understand the situation, the relationship, the transaction at a different level and then see ourselves in a different light. We must be willing to see and accept ourselves and the other person realistically and not deny the person's human limitations, motivations, and agendas. We must learn not to give away our own power. We must learn to protect ourselves from further hurt and repetition.

Forgiveness work has less to do with the person we are forgiving than with ourselves. How are we becoming free? If we are not able or willing to forgive ourselves, we are being held in bondage to the past, to the power of others, to our less-than-fully developed selves.

What is essential, then, is that we learn how to release ourselves from this inner bondage. Equally important, we must hold no one else in bondage to us, however heinous the heartbreak or offense. What is essential is that we also learn to accept God's forgiveness in our lives.

Today, those involved in spiritual direction, spiritual growth, psychotherapy, or journaling can assist us in forgiveness work. There are many good books that also provide effective tools for use in this work. *Forgiveness: How To Make Peace With Your Past and Get On With Your Life,* by Dr. Sidney B. Simon and Suzanne Simon, makes a substantial contribution to this work.

I want also to suggest that you take time to write your own eulogy. It is usually a remarkably meaningful exercise for most people who do so. In some ways, it allows you to complete some unfinished business, grow in gratitude for the life you live, and sharpen your perspective for what remains of earthly life.

As you write, consider the following questions for yourself:

- What lessons did you learn in your life?
- What do you feel you did not master or complete?
- What were your major values that you cherished and upheld?
- What messages do you want to leave with others?
- What was the meaning of your life?
- How did your relationship and understanding of God unfold?
- How did you delight in the gift of life?

In writing your eulogy to be read at your funeral, consider privacy; make this a personal time between you and God. What you want to avoid, of course, is reading it to a relative or friend and asking them, "How does this sound to you?" Remember you are not seeking to create an image. This is soul work. I want to encourage you to make it a private, soul experience between you and God. As the months and years pass, it will be necessary to make some changes in your eulogy as you grow and your life changes.

What, then, is life review? It is what the term implies. It is a process whereby we see and explore and then judge the history and meaning of earthly life

in the presence of God, in the presence of the Being of
God, the Holy Spirit, and for Christians, also in the
presence of Christ.

Many years ago when I was engaged in full-time
college teaching I showed a film strip series to the
students in my death and dying classes. It concerned
itself with the question of judgment at the time of
death—an area of concern in all religious traditions.
This is visually a most impressive filmstrip, and I am
not able to do it justice here. It presented a young adult
man who, after his death, came into the presence of
God, Divine Love, Light, Justice, and Mercy. In the
presence of the Divine, little pictures of his life flashed
continuously before him. He, together with God, was
to review these and then make a judgment. As these
pictures flashed before him, several questions had to
be answered.

- How did I love myself and others?
- How did I hurt myself and others?
- How did I use/misuse my talents and vocation?
- How did I seek God and develop my relationship
  with God?
- How did I value and enjoy life?

In light of that judgment, the young man's progress
was decided.

I am reminded, as I write, of an experience I had in

1996. A colleague of mine, who in her earlier years had been a member of my bereavement support group, died after a long bout with cancer. I was not able to attend her funeral, but I did have some correspondence with her when she was first diagnosed. About a week after her funeral while I was on my daily walk, Toni came to me and apologized for not following through on a special request I had made of her some ten years earlier. It surprised me initially, because I had forgotten it completely and it was not a problem for me at all. Apparently it was still important to Toni. As I reflected I remembered that at the time I had been very disappointed and felt hurt. It was clear to me that Toni was in life review. Of course, I forgave her and of course, I expressed my gratitude to her for the many blessings she brought to me in life.

When we look at the imagery of the kabbala in the Jewish tradition, we see that the Angel of Death meets a person during this transition. At this point, a person is asked:

- Who are you, what is your essence?
- How did you/did you not develop yourself?
- Why did you not enjoy the permissible delights of this world?
- What are you still attached to in earthly life?

All attachment to the physical must be released.

Images of judgment appear. Good deeds and evil deeds are weighed. Purification of the soul must take place, if evolution is to take place. Many questions must be answered. They relate to what in the soul needs yet to be learned, to be completed, to be transformed, to be educated, and to be repaired.

Why is life review work important? Because it adds to the dignity of each of us as a person and also honors our spiritual identity and relationship with God. This result is important because movement requires accountability, and when we die and cross over (when we make our transition) and awaken to life on the other side, transformation takes place.

Think for one moment, if you will, of a loving and devoted mother meeting again her darling child who died in infancy or youth. Think of the indescribable joy, delight, love, and healing transformation that takes place for both of them.

Crossing over carries with it changes. Crossing over means facing and letting go of our illusions and attachments and taking hold of and participating in a higher life of love, joy, freedom, truth, discovery, beauty, and wisdom. Crossing over means entering more fully into the glory of God at whatever level we are able to absorb and understand.

What is it that needs to be unlearned, what repair

work needs to be made? Often a person dies chained
and paralyzed by thoughts and feelings of bitterness,
evil, fear, rebellion, resentment, selfishness, and vindic-
tiveness. Often a person dies with a lack of faith,
compassion, spiritual understanding, and spiritual
motivation. All of these lapses in love, faith, and
conscience must be recognized and rectified before any
soul progress can be made. Remorse, forgiveness, faith,
and resignation are essential for soul growth.

In a culture and time when accountability is not
always in vogue, these realities do not ring true for
many people. How sad that is! As a spiritual person
one cannot ascend to higher spheres of learning,
beauty, love, joy, creativity, and divine purpose without honest effort and response to grace. We cannot
enter into higher levels of divine relationship, harmony, and freedom or union with the Divine and
conscious awareness of our heritage without desire for
God and response to God's grace.

God's grace is ever operative. There is no insuffi-
ciency with God. God offers help through more refined
souls, spiritual teachers, healers, and helpers for those
chained in ignorance, mesmerized by illusion, satisfied
with arrogant self-centeredness, and satiated with
hatefulness. Cleansing must begin before significant
movement occurs.

As our consciousness is purified and expands, we are able to absorb more light. We learn to commune with the Divine and channel Divine life, love, and activity through the spheres and God's universe. Progress on the other side depends on many factors, some known to us, some mysterious. At the very least, it depends on our perception and openness to the Spirit of God and to Divine Life, also upon our ability and willingness to embrace light, peace, joy, and love. Most important, it depends on our ability and willingness to love, serve, and to be in mission in God's heavenly kingdom.

Traditionally, when we address the subject of judgment at death, we lock ourselves into understanding judgment to mean eternal damnation or eternal reward.

In many of today's mainline church communities when we speak seriously of eternity, we do so more in terms of progressive union. That is, at an eternal level, we embrace an evolutionary perspective in the development of our union with God. I am aware, however, that there are many mainline conservative and fundamentalist churches that do not accept this perspective of eternity. For those of you interested in the conservative or fundamentalist position, I recommend Joni Eareckson Tada's book, *Heaven—Your Real Home,* and

Dr. Charles F. Stanley's book, *Eternal Security: Can You Be Sure?*, or his audiotape series, *The Judgments of Revelation.*

Divine judgment is certainly part of the process, but rather than pronouncing damnation—meaning that a spirit person is damned forever, with no possibility of ever moving in that process—we talk rather of accountability and purification. Each of us is accountable for who we are, what we are, and what we did and did not do. Each of us is accountable for our choices, our knowledge, our learning opportunities.

What of hell? All major religions speak of hell at some level. Jesus speaks also of hell. I, too, recognize the reality of hell. However, when I make reference to hell I am not referring to a hell in which souls are eternally damned, mentally and spiritually, with no possibility of God's grace reaching into that.

God's grace is capable of reaching into every aspect of our eternal journey. Hell is for those who are so fixated themselves they have been and are still unwilling to respond to God's grace—souls so consumed with demonic, negative energy they know no way other than greed, hate, abusive power, and wickedness.

Rev. Alan Jones, Dean of San Francisco's Grace Cathedral (Episcopal), writes in his fascinating book, *The Soul's Journey,* that hell is the place where the self

becomes its own contemptuous god devouring itself
and never being satisfied.

We also know that there are any number of spiritual helpers, healers, and teachers anointed by God to
approach and work with the tormented, complacent,
and hideous. These are God's vessels, who try to
awaken and teach spirits how to think, to forgive, and
to overcome rejection of all that is Divine.

What are we asked to do? Respond. That is the
change in thinking and direction and movement today.
As we recognize who we are as spirit persons, we
recognize to whom we belong and for what purposes
we are being fashioned eternally.

The sacred scriptures refer to the soul as "a living
soul" that will survive the death of the body and will
be given eternal life. Rev. Ephraim Eaton, writing in
Our Friends Immortal, tells us, "It is not likely that the
soul that is loyal to the Redeemer will ever come to the
end of its journey, neither in this life nor in that which
is to come."[5]

Over the last fifty years a great resurgence of
attention and dialogue has been given to the doctrine
of immortality. Whereas this doctrine has defined the
faith of the Christian community, there has been a
difference in interpretation within the community.

Some Christians believe and teach that when an

individual dies, he is buried body and soul in the grave where he awaits the resurrection. Other Christians believe and teach that when an individual dies, only his body is buried in the grave, and the souls of saints are welcomed into heaven, where they remain until the resurrection and general judgment. Much of recent cross-denominational discussion of these matters, however, speaks of death as a time when saints are received into Paradise. "Paradise," Rev. Eaton writes, "is both a state and place of life provided for all the children of God, and where they will continue, in peace and happiness, and probably in growth and preparation for the larger life, which they shall enter after the resurrection and general judgment."[6]

Heaven is the home of God, the eternal dwelling place of the soul and the future life to which the children of God are called.

Carroll E. Simcox, Episcopalian priest and former editor of *The Living Church,* in his deeply penetrating book *The Eternal You*, expands our understanding of eternity even further. He writes:

> If God loves us as our Father, he wants ourselves to be his forever. And ourselves cannot be selves unless they are conscious: God-conscious, other-conscious, self-conscious. . . .[Instead of] an extinction of personal consciousness at death, I expect an inconceivable heightening and enhancement of it.

"The soul is a hollow which God fills," as C. S. Lewis writes in *The Problem of Pain.*

We grow in being as God feeds and fills us with the life eternal. He fills this "hollow" so that we can love him and join him in loving his world, as servants of that love in worlds we have not yet traversed and which may still be waiting to be born .[7]

As God nourishes us and calls us into the fullness of His love, we grow in spiritual stature and, in turn, feed others in our world. As we express this love and service we are made ready and more complete to embrace eternal life in the world beyond.

Mary Baker Eddy, discoverer and founder of Christian Science, writing in *Science and Health with Key to the Scriptures,* states: ". . . to understand God is the work of eternity and demands absolute consecration of thought, energy and desire."[8] She is correct.

Knowing and understanding more of the spirit world beyond death, more of the eternal heritage God has in mind for us, helps to feed and strengthen our human pilgrimage and commitment and purposes on Earth. Spirituality is not magic nor an appendage in human experience. Spirituality isn't an exercise in supernatural piety. Spirituality offers illumination for our path. It is concerned rather with the human hunger for meaning, value, love and purpose. It helps each one of us to recognize the ultimate mystery of consciousness. It causes us to search and order and direct and interpret our experience. Spirituality rightly used is a loving and unifying energy in our lives.

Each of the world's religious traditions seeks to shape the character of its people as they attain soul realization. As a committed Christian, I seek to live my own life in an ever deepening, wise, and loving surrender to the Spirit of Christ. I seek to know, understand, develop, and demonstrate the consciousness of Christ within my being and becoming. It is for me a learning process, requiring humility and discernment and forgiveness. It is an eternal process rooted and grounded in my day-to-day earthly life. It is a process and a relationship in which I try to integrate spiritual disciplines, the eternal promises of God and the mystical experiences that God grants to me throughout my journey; a journey that is complete with its very human strengths and weaknesses, joys and sorrows, successes and failures, defeats and victories, frustrations and satisfactions.

Phillip Keller helps us to recognize and appreciate the interchange of the life of the Spirit within us in his book *A Shepherd Looks At the Good Shepherd and His Sheep.* It is through our intuition and our conscience that we are able to commune with the Spirit of the Living God.

When we remain active in our desire to commune with the Lord, He comes to energize and uplift us in His life and love. This is intended, from the beginning of our own lives, to be an eternal relationship. In this interchange Keller encourages us to be open so as not to impede the flow of God's life within us, and to practice patience so that God's finest plans will unfold.[9]

Again, let me call your attention to Simcox's book *The Eternal You,* in which he writes:

> The theme with variations of this book is a conviction, a passionate intuition, which may be simply stated: You, I, all human beings, indeed all things, animate and inanimate, visible and invisible, are eternal. You existed in the mind of God—therefore you existed before time and the world began. You exist in God now, you will exist in God forever, as will everybody and everything. A million years ago you existed and were being created prenatally. You were not yet incarnate and you had no self awareness, but God was creating you and knowing exactly what he was doing, and making no mistakes, no matter what you may think or fear. He will be creating you a million years from now in a dimension of being in which time is not measured by years and space is not measured by miles.[10]

Yes, we are accountable in and for our human journey. Yes, we participate in judgment after death with the God of our being. Yes, hell is a reality. Yes, there is an individual progressive unfoldment of Heaven. Yes, we are asked to value and respond to God's Grace.

Dr. Leslie Weatherhead, London United Methodist Bishop, is known and celebrated for his book *The Will of God*. In another of his books, *Life Begins at Death,* he raises several questions relevant to all of us.[11]

Would you say that we develop in life after death?
Oh, definitely. If there is life there must be growth. There can't be a thing called the static soul in another life any more than in this life. . . .

What [do you say] about little children who die before religion has any meaning at all?
I can only suggest that at death we go on spiritually where we left off.

This then applies to the child who dies in infancy and has had no opportunity for soul growth; he goes on from where he left off?
Yes, and if you say he left off before he could have made any spiritual progress, surely there are helpers waiting for him on the other side. . . .

Would you say that we sinners get a second chance [for soul growth]?
Not only a second chance but a thousand chances. If the soul goes on where it left off and still has free will, it has the power of choice. It can make the choice of climbing higher, or it can make the choice of indifference, or it can make the choice of descending lower. . . .

And now we must ask ourselves, "What is the place of prayer in this phase of our journey?" Prayer is a powerful and lovely channel of communication with the Divine, for opening us to God's light, for experiencing the presence and power of God. It is also a powerful connection between the Earth world and the eternal world. Prayer impacts those who have died and moved on. The prayer-thought energy of eternal spirits living in the world beyond, on our behalf, can also have a positive impact.

After my father's death in 1971, I spent one day each month in fasting, prayer, and acts of love for his benefit. I fasted also on the anniversary of his death and on his birthday. I did the same for my brother, Michael, who died at age twenty-eight in 1979. In my dialogue with God I would say simply, "Lord, I cannot give them a gift today. Please accept this from me for their greater good in their new life. Thank you for your grace now moving them into greater life, love, and happiness in your heavenly kingdom."

Several years ago, a colleague and most refreshing friend of mine died and passed on. Margot was spiritually advanced. We shared deeply through our many years of friendship. I remember her even now for her laughter and her joy. By her own admission, she confided to me her greatest spiritual struggle was with impatience. She revealed to me many situations in her life that she felt were very costly and had blocked her development and response to God. I remembered that after she died. Through the first year following her death, I committed here on the Earth to practice and develop greater patience (sometimes in excruciatingly difficult situations) for her greater unfoldment and development in eternity. I simply shared with the Lord my intent and surrendered it.

To my grievers dealing with a suicide in the family, I recommend that they identify what made their loved ones so vulnerable. Once this is done, I encourage them to dialogue with God and in some way practice here on Earth what they know their loved one needed to learn and grow in spiritually. In our own journeys here, I believe, we can offer continuing teaching and encouragement to those on the other side of life.

In this discussion and exploration of Divine judgment and human accountability, let me be very emphatic about the fact that God is not indifferent to evil or our evil intentions or behavior. Let me be very clear in stating that abject evil can and does confuse and paralyze a soul in the eternal journey.

Think, for just a moment, of those times in your earthly life in which you were, perhaps, not moving or responding to the grace of God. In spite of your awareness of the attempts on the part of others to help you, or circumstances to change your direction, you still resisted or remained apathetic or indifferent. As you reflect on your life and history so far, how long did it take you finally to surrender, grow, change, and integrate a new way, attitude, or practice? How long did it take you to make the right decision or choice, release the paralyzing habit, overcome the compulsion? It isn't always smooth or easy, or once and for all, is it?

Similar questions must be asked of those living in darkness on the other side. How long does it take to unlearn and relearn? How long does it take to respond mentally and spiritually? What is the mental and spiritual purification process? How long does it take to see the light of God and embrace it?

We surely do not want to trivialize the sovereignty of God and the love of God or our importance to God and our responsibilities to God. We surely do not want to trivialize the gift of human life and earthly experience. Our God-given capacity to experience and understand the eternal realms or the life of the soul are far too precious to be treated lightly.

CHAPTER SIX

DEATHBED VISIONS AND TRANSITIONS

Another phase of our awakening to after-death communication centers in deathbed visions. Hospice workers, in particular, can attest to some profound patterns of interaction and awareness that take place with their patients at the time of death. Many compassionate and well-experienced hospital chaplains and congregational pastors and rabbis can do likewise.

I'm sure that many of you reading this book can share similar stories of participating in the death of a loved one who claimed to see the face of a relative or hear the voice of one who had already died.

In the preface to his book *Voices from the Edge of Eternity,* Dr. John Myers tells us that inadvertently he found a resourceful and illuminating book of deathbed testimonies published as early as 1898. The book featured a wide variety of people: professional, religious and nonreligious, including both old and young, female and male, the virtuous and nonvirtuous. What was common to all, however, was the clear vision of what was to come after they died. For example, when the president of Wake Forest College, Dr. Washington Manley Wingate, lay dying, those gathered around him heard him personally talking to the Master as follows:

> "Oh, how delightful it is! I knew you would be with me when the time came, and I knew it would be sweet— but not as sweet as it is!"[1]

Myers adds that Elizabeth Barrett Browning, famous English poet who expressed faith in Christ throughout her life and work, is reported to have spoken as her last words: "It is beautiful!"[2]

Myers also includes a relevant account given by Norman Vincent Peale of the conversation he had with the late Mrs. Thomas A. Edison, who told him of the last moments of her husband's life. Her famous husband as he was dying whispered to his physician, "It is very beautiful over there." Edison was one of the world's greatest scientists who committed his life's energy to investigation and discovery. He was objective and factual. He relied on evidence to prove his facts. Dr. Peale writes that Edison would never have reported, "It is very beautiful over there" unless, having seen, he knew it to be true.[3]

Moreover, as Myers adds, the author Ann Knight expressed similar revelations the night she died in 1806: "I have seen Heaven, and they are all happy, so happy there." She reported feeling the presence of the Almighty. She heeded this call to let go of the earthly and take hold of the heavenly happiness and peace she had seen.[4]

In 1989 my Aunt Connie called to tell me that my Uncle Ed was hospitalized in serious condition in Massachusetts. The next day when I phoned to inquire about him, she told me that he was holding his own, but that he kept telling her he was seeing his brother, Francis, at the foot of his bed. Francis was my father, who died in 1971. She said, "I told him, 'Eddy, you've never talked crazy in all of your life, please don't start now.'" As she talked, I was hearing a message from my father. I said, "Aunt Connie, don't do that. Tell Uncle Ed it's all right for him to take his brother's visit seriously. He's bringing him love and comfort." The next day she called to tell me he died, in a spirit of love, with all his family by his bedside.

Those who have a relationship in their lifetime with Jesus or Mary or one of the saints or a Yoga

Master often see them at the time of their death. It is important that we recognize and allow ourselves to respond to the energy coming near to us to prepare us to make the transition. No one ever dies alone. Billy Graham in his book *Angels: God's Secret Agents,* shares a story concerning his maternal grandmother. When she died, he said that her room seemed to be filled with a heavenly light. "She sat up in bed and almost laughingly said, 'I see Jesus. He has His arms outstretched toward me. I see Ben [her husband who died years earlier], and I see the angels.' She then slumped over, absent from the body but present with the Lord."[5]

Louis XVII, King of France, is reported as having said, as he lay dying in 1551, that he heard beautiful music that relieved his suffering, and in the midst of many voices he recognized his mother's.[6]

When John Wesley, the founder of Methodism, was nearing death, one of his congregation members recalls his dying words:

> We knelt down and truly our hearts were filled with the Divine Presence; the room seemed to be filled with God. . . . After a pause he summoned all his strength and cried out, "The best of all, God is with us."[7]

An interesting story appears in the book *Gifts: Two Hospice Professionals Reveal Messages From Those Passing On,*

written by Anne Wallace Sharp and Susan Handle
Terbay. The story was submitted by Dee Baughman, a
social worker, at the time of her father's death. It gives
us some insight into the reciprocity that sometimes
occurs when one is participating in the death experience of another.

   . . . Dee had been told by her father's physician that he
had pancreatic cancer and had only a couple of weeks to
live. Her mom had died earlier in her life. She and her
dad had shared an especially supportive and loving
relationship. The news was devastating for her. Her dad
seemed to hear this painful news with strength, and
sometimes he even showed some excitement about going
to heaven and being reunited with her mom.

   In the days that followed, her dad seemed already to
be in contact with the next world. He reported hearing
harmonious music. Dee could not. He seemed to be in
private enjoyable conversation with others in the room.
One time he asked Dee, "I don't suppose you saw the
lady with the purple dress come in and just sit at the head
of the bed, did you?"

   Dee, of course, did not. Nonetheless, Dee was aware
that something authentic was happening privately for her
father. Her dad reported other heavenly presences to her,
who daily brought a gentle support to him during those
weeks. Though she didn't experience any of this directly,
she believed her dad, without any hesitation.

The day before her father died she writes, "Daddy told me that I had guided his spirit so it would be ready to depart this world."

The following year she was hired to work at the Hospice. It was during that time she realized "With Daddy's spirit guiding me, I help others make their final life journey."[8]

Dr. Leslie Weatherhead writes in *Life Begins at Death* that he sat at the bedside of a dying man who was conscious to the end. "He gripped my hand and I must have gripped his more tightly than I thought I was doing, for he said, 'Don't hold me back. I can see through the gates. It's marvelous.'"[9]

Not unlike the reports of other hospital chaplains, Dr. Weatherhead shares some very convincing deathbed experiences. One of these involved a woman so frail that she was unable to lift her head from the pillow. Nonetheless, just before she died, he witnessed her "sit up [in bed], her eyes open with tremendous delight and joy in her face, [and] call the name of a beloved husband who had been dead twenty years."

Among Dr. Weatherhead's own family members, his father-in-law had much to teach him about these matters. When he was dying he spoke continually of the presence of his daughter. She had been dead for many years.

Among his colleagues, Dr. Weatherhead speaks of a sister affiliated with a large university hospital. She had the care of a terminally ill woman. During the course of her dying, this woman's son, unknown to his mother, had committed suicide. The woman said to the sister, "Do you know Michael has been with me all day today?"

Because the woman was unaware that her son had taken his own life, she was not simply imagining things. Both the sister and Dr. Weatherhead believed that Michael was very likely near to his mother.[10]

Dr. Karlis Osis, a native of Riga, Latvia, worked with Dr. Joseph Banks Rhine at Duke University on ESP and precognition. He later became research director at the Parapsychology Foundation in New York. Dr. Osis developed a great interest in deathbed visions and circulated a questionnaire to doctors and nurses asking them what they had observed about dying patients. Six hundred and forty questionnaires were returned, covering more than 35,000 cases. In 1961, Osis published *Deathbed Observations by Physicians and Nurses.* The most consistently reported feature of this research is that of "seeing" and holding conversations with deceased friends and relatives whom no one else present could either see or hear.

What are we to make of the communication, both

symbolic and direct, that takes place in the days
immediately following a death?
Ram Dass, in *Grist for the Mill,* talks of his mother's
funeral.

> For forty-four years my mother and father on their
> anniversary had exchanged, along with gifts, one red rose
> that was a token of their love for one another. At the
> temple the casket was covered with a blanket of roses. As
> the casket was wheeled out of the temple, it came by the
> first pew. In the first pew were seated my father, at the
> time a Boston Republican lawyer in his mid-sixties, ex-
> president of a railroad, very conservative; my oldest
> brother, a stockbroker-lawyer, my middle brother, also a
> lawyer, but one who was having spiritual experiences,
> me, and sisters-in-law. As the coffin went by the first pew,
> one rose from the blanket of roses fell at the feet of my
> father. All of us in the pew looked at the rose. We all
> knew the story of the exchange of one rose, but of course
> nobody said anything. As we left the pew my father
> picked up the rose and was holding it as we sat in the
> limousine. Finally, my brother said, "She sent you a last
> message," and everybody in the car at that moment
> agreed. Everybody said, "Yes!" The emotion of the
> moment sanctioned an acceptance of a reality totally alien
> to at least three members of the group.[11]

On September 19, 1997, I was awakened at 4 A.M.
with the name of William Downey in my conscious-

ness. I arose and spent the next hour in prayer and scripture meditation and poetry reading with Bill in mind. I had often done this during the previous five months as he struggled with pancreatic cancer. During those five months I had no direct, physical contact or visitation with Bill. I communicated with him through letters and cards or in meditation to bring comfort to him and share my wisdom with him.

At noon, when I returned from a morning of college teaching, I was informed that Bill had died at dawn that day. Shortly after, a dear and sensitive friend and coworker phoned to make arrangements with me to attend Bill's memorial service on Monday at 4 P.M.

My thought and conversation with friends and colleagues centered on Bill all that day. Saturday, I was feeling sad but kept quite busy most of the day. About 3:30 P.M., while I was driving, I was thinking how much I was dreading seeing Bill in his casket. At that very moment, he came to me and said, "But, Jacqui, I'm not in that casket." I said, "I know that, but I have to work out this grief." I was not aware of any further contact with him during the weekend until his visitation late Monday afternoon.

When I arrived, I had the opportunity to dialogue with Patrick, his youngest son, about the circumstances of Bill's death. My friend Beverly and I then entered the lounge area and were greeted by his beloved wife, Dorothy, who said, "I think Bill would have been pleased with all of these arrangements." We agreed. When I approached his casket, I reached out to touch his hand and wish him God's continuing peace and love. As I did, I felt his energy to the right above the casket. He signaled me and I felt the wonderful freedom and harmony of his spirit. As I continued to move among his family and friends to pay condolences, Bill's presence became known to me again as I talked with his wife. Because of my childcare responsibilities that day, I could not stay during the dinner hour, so I returned home.

The next morning, I arrived early and had the opportunity to spend a few minutes of private time with Bill in the Chapel of the Chimes. Later, his memorial service proceeded and was a fitting tribute to him. All of his children honored him, each in turn. About midpoint in the service I was again aware of Bill's presence. He was standing behind me for a few minutes and then moved on.

Though totally unexpected, my experience of Bill's presence and communication was very enlightening. When we attended the luncheon following his service, I became aware of him again.

Eight of us were discussing the pros and cons of writing our own memorial services. I heard Bill clearly say to me, "It's more responsible and authentic to plan your own beforehand." He remained at our table through the luncheon.

Before leaving the Family Center at Wisconsin Memorial Park I was engaged in conversation with Bill's oldest son, Bill Jr., when Bill came in behind his son and remained there during our short conversation. During that time I felt a new peacefulness from him. I left the Family Center and returned home. I spent the next four hours writing my own memorial service, peacefully, proudly, and effortlessly. Though I had attempted to do so several times during the previous year, I had been unable to find the energy to organize it or make any worthwhile progress with it.

Some seven years ago, I talked with a remarkable woman at our church who was diagnosed with liver cancer. Elizabeth was a courageous woman, intelligent and generous. Her encounter with terminal illness was life-transforming for her. Her love deepened, her faith expanded. She came to value gentleness in a new way and honor the meaning and power of forgiveness in her life and in the lives of others. Elizabeth was perceptive. She touched the lives and destiny of her husband and children in many precious ways.

In the weeks preceding her death, we spent several hours together deep in thought and feeling related to her dying experience and eternity. Elizabeth valued deeply and authentically her relationship with Christ and the beauty and strength of her Christian faith. I had real respect for her. I was not, however, with her at the time of her death.

Altogether, I had four after-death experiences of Elizabeth over a six-month period. The most memorable occurred at her memorial service. Several hundred people attended. Elizabeth very lovingly and carefully wrote and planned her own service. It proceeded as planned, and I was attentive. As soon as Rev. Jones began to speak of Elizabeth and her life and her manifold contributions, Elizabeth passed in front of me and then moved to the right of me. She remained slightly in front of me to the right until the pastor finished speaking. Then she left. While Elizabeth was present, I felt keenly the overflowing joy in her spirit as she made contact with me. Not before had I experienced such wonderful joy as I did with Elizabeth. Joy and elevation came through her very clearly. She indeed had reason to be joyful. She had nourished so many with her dedication and life.

Nearly five years ago, I had lunch with Adele, a woman three times widowed in her lifetime. She was a very wealthy woman and the mother of eight children. She was also a peace activist, worldwide traveler and leading benefactor in our community. Adele was a vivacious, intelligent woman, well loved by those who knew her. That day and on several other occasions over the following two years I attempted to dialogue with her related to the afterlife and eternity. I was unsuccessful.

There were many reasons for this. Adele was a busy woman, committed to her causes. There was some resistance on her part to a subject of this kind. Further, there always seemed to be some interference or distraction from the outside to prevent us from finding the right time or place. I thought it would be better not to pressure her with this and let the opportunity unfold more naturally.

Without warning, Adele died at home alone in the summer of 1993. I attended her church service but didn't attend the luncheon that followed, provided by her family, due to conflicting commitments.

Later that afternoon, I took time for prayer, reading, and journaling at a nearby church garden. As I was preparing to spread my blanket on the lawn, I felt Adele's energy. As I looked up, she came to me and said, "I want to tell you something. I should have listened to you." Then she left. I quietly reflected on this and was encouraged. It was the one and only experience I had of Adele, but it was very meaningful and helpful to me in my work. In her own way, she taught me the importance of that work. Now, when I feel called to share death-related experiences, I am no longer timid and I don't allow myself to tolerate too many excuses.

In the prologue to his book, *Parting Visions,* Dr. Melvin Morse writes of a vision shared by two people, simultaneously, that occurred at the death of a boy named Jimmy.[12]

The supernatural story begins in the most natural of ways. Around Valentine's Day, Elizabeth was busy helping a little boy die. He had a form of heart disease, and the doctors had done everything they could to prolong his life. Now that the end was near, this boy—we will call him Jimmy—had decided to die at home.

His parents supported his decision to die at home. They had seen him struggle for a long time, and they knew it was his time to die. They surrounded him with love and tried to make his last days as comfortable as possible.

Elizabeth, his hospice nurse came to help. She frequently found herself visiting people's homes, where she administered medicine to the dying and gave the family some rest from the strain of caring for the terminally ill.

Elizabeth took a special liking to Jimmy and his family. They were tightknit and caring, and Jimmy showed much of the confidence and intelligence of a child who was raised by supportive parents.

Jimmy and his family gave everything they had to each other in his last days. They celebrated his ninth birthday on Valentine's Day, a few months early, because they knew he wouldn't make it to the actual date. His only birthday wish was to go to dinner in a limousine. Although they were poor, Jimmy's parents did the best they could, renting a black Lincoln because they couldn't afford an actual limo. The whole family rode around town as Jimmy basked in the front seat of the car.

He liked the car and said that he wished he could buy one for his family. When they stopped for dinner, it was at a convenience market, where they ate hotdogs and drank Slurpees. For awhile it was as though he had forgotten that this was his last birthday party.

Later he wrote Valentine notes to all his friends. In the envelopes he enclosed tiny gold crosses he had purchased and asked that they be used to remember him by.

The actual death a few weeks later was not a surprise. His mother said that he got up early that morning to make sandwiches for his brothers' school lunches. "I want to make sure their sandwiches are special today," he told his mother. "They are going to need all of the energy they can get."

Jimmy weakened as the day progressed. He went into the living room to lie down. He asked that his favorite music be put on his tape player as he lay there. The fight was fading out of his eyes by then. Elizabeth could see it was Jimmy's time to let go and die. She monitored his vital signs and gave him what aid and comfort she could.

By sundown Jimmy was actively dying. His heartbeat was fluctuating, and there were periods where he seemed to slip into a coma.

Elizabeth marveled at how much dying resembled the birthing process. Music was playing, and the parents embraced Jimmy. "Come on," they said. "Come on, now, it's all right, Jimmy. It's okay to let go." For a moment Jimmy would seem to leave his body. Then he would pull back, and the spark of life would show again on his face. Finally he became weaker and weaker as his parents held him closer. Then he sighed and left his body for good, surrounded by his brothers, parents, pediatrician, and Elizabeth.

Elizabeth's job was almost over.

She helped the family make some of the necessary phone calls and waited for the mortuary van to arrive. When she noticed that one of Jimmy's brothers was standing alone in the front yard, she took a basketball outside and shot hoops with him to help him feel better. About half an hour later she left for home.

That was when it happened.

As she drove down the freeway, the windshield was suddenly filled with a vision so vivid that she had to pull off to the side of the road.

In this vision she saw Jimmy, happy and animated, holding a man's hand. She couldn't see whose hand he was holding, but Jimmy was happy. He looked adoringly toward the man's face and had a look of great peace. The vision was as real as a moving picture and continued for as long as one minute. No words were spoken by the boy, but his eyes said it all as far as Elizabeth was concerned. "The life was back in his bright blue eyes and he was very comfortable," said Elizabeth. "I could hear him say, 'I'm all right now,' without moving his lips."

Elizabeth told only her husband about the vision. She thought of keeping it that way, but what she had seen was so vivid that she felt she had to tell someone else. She thought she should at least tell Jimmy's family. Certainly they would find comfort in what she had seen.

After the funeral Elizabeth pulled Jimmy's mother aside. They were standing outside the cemetery next to a tree when Elizabeth told the mother what she had seen. The woman immediately burst into tears.

"That's exactly what my husband saw," she said. "Right after Jimmy died, my husband saw the same thing."

CHAPTER SEVEN

EXTRASENSORY PERCEPTION

Parapsychology is the science that lies "beside" or "beyond" psychology. It studies those unique experiences and unknown capabilities of the human mind that suggest consciousness has the potential for interacting with the physical world in ways not yet recognized by science but not beyond science's ability to investigate.

Parapsychologists refer to ESP—extrasensory perception—as a process that manifests itself as precognition, clairvoyance, clairaudience, or telepathy.

I'd like to define these terms.

Precognition: to know beforehand

Clairvoyance: to "see" in one's mind faces, symbols, objects, figures, places, events, letters, or numbers.

Clairaudience: the power or faculty of hearing some
                 things not present to the ear, but regarded
                 as having objective reality.

Telepathy: apparent communication from one mind
                 to another other than through the channel
                 of sense.

Research in these areas started in 1882 in England
with the Society for Psychical Research (SPR) and the
first publication of its proceedings in 1883.

In the United States, Dr. Joseph Banks Rhine and
his wife, Dr. Louisa E. Rhine, established their Parapsychology Laboratory as an autonomous unit on the
campus of Duke University in 1935.

The Parapsychological Association was officially
accepted as an affiliate member of the American
Association for the Advancement of Science (AAAS) in
1969. Parapsychological research and investigation
must adhere to the same criteria required of any
scientific research.

Today the Duke University Parapsychology Laboratory has been succeeded by the Rhine Research
Center, a nonprofit research and educational organization committed to carrying forward the famed
laboratory's research mission and educational programs.

The American Society for Psychical Research

(ASPR) in New York, the Parapsychology Foundation
also in New York, and the Exceptional Human Experience Network in North Carolina are among the thriv-
ing parapsychological research and information
centers in the United States today.

Many examples illustrate and support this kind of
investigation. The following is vouched for by the late
Professor J.B. Rhine.

To the students of extra-sensory perception (ESP), the
most significant type of case history where the question
of survival is concerned is one in which the information
transmitted to the living person was known only to the
deceased, or one in which the *method* of transmission is
beyond the capabilities of the person through whom the
information comes.

A professor at Northwestern University received the
following case from one of his students which is notewor-
thy on both counts.

"One evening when I was a boy of four, before I knew
anything of school or the alphabet, my mother was
working at her desk in our hotel, and I got hold of a note
pad and began scribbling on it. Mother, noticing what I
was doing, told me to stop and play with something else.

"The next morning my mother saw the papers with my
scribbling and was about to throw them away when the
day clerk, who had taken shorthand at night school, told
her they looked like shorthand. He insisted on taking the

papers to a teacher for examination. They *were* shorthand,
the old-fashioned square-type shorthand.

On those papers was a message to my mother from my
father who had died two weeks before in New York while
my mother and I were in Oregon. It started, "Dearest
Beloved," and spoke of a letter that had not been posted.
It was an urgent letter containing information about
father's safety deposit box in the East. His death had been
sudden, and mother had not known the location of that
box.

My father had always called my mother "Dearest
Beloved," and as a young man had learned the old-
fashioned method of shorthand. Mother still has those
pieces of paper, and the message has been verified by
other people, too.[1]

Understandably, such an experience does not satis-
fy a scientist's search for proof of life after death. It
does, however, help support scientific research which
recognizes something within man that reflects a set of
properties different from those of the physical body.
This recognition makes survival a logical possibility.

In his invaluable book *The Medium, the Mystic, and the
Physicist,* Lawrence LeShan discusses the similarities
between the clairvoyant reality shared by the mystic
and the medium, and the picture of reality given by
modern physics.

According to Dr. LeShan, there are four central

aspects of the clairvoyant reality:

1. There is a central unity to all things. The most important aspect of a "thing" is its relationships, its part in the whole. Its individuality and separateness are secondary and/or illusory.

2. Pastness, presentness, and futurity are illusions we project onto the "seamless garment" of time. There is another valid view of time in which these separations do not exist.

3. From this other view of the world, evil is mere appearance: when we are in this other understanding (a term which originally meant to "stand under," "to be a part of"), we do not judge with the criteria of good and evil.

4. There is a better way of gaining information than through the senses.[2]

I believe many people of the nonmystical mode look skeptically, to say the least, at this aspect of reality. However, its mark in the lives of the learned overthrows the belief that only nonmystical states of experiences are sufficient to define reality.

Evelyn Underhill, one of the most profound and serious mystics of this century, makes it clear in her excellent book, *Mysticism,* that the mystic relates to and writes with a different conceptualization of reality than the one we ordinarily use.

The distinction between mystic and nonmystic is not merely that between the rationalist and the dreamer, between intellect and intuition. The question which divides them is really this: what, out of the mass of material offered it, shall consciousness seize upon— with what aspect of the universe shall it "unite"?

Carroll Simcox also reflects the importance of the mystic in *The Eternal You.* He explains that he quotes from poets more than theologians, because, for him, they are more authoritative.

> A poet or mystic "sees" a truth by feeling it, yet not merely by feeling it. If he is intelligent, as all good poets and mystics are, he unceasingly inspects his feelings with his mind and his conscience. His feelings are intuitions, passionate and yet rational and moral. He trusts them as guides to truth and still more as messengers of truth from truth. The conventional philosopher or theologian does not trust his feelings in such a way.[3]

I discovered Evelyn Underhill on my own in 1969 and relished her work. I studied and absorbed all that I could for the following ten years. Evelyn was a practitioner of mysticism. In her very person, she epitomized how she described practitioners of this "art of union with reality."All higher civilizations produce at times curious personality types dissatisfied with the commonly perceived outlook and ready to deny the world so as to find reality. In whatever place or period they arise, doctrines and methods are substantially the same. Such individuals' experience, curiously self-consistent and often mutually explanatory, must be taken into account in considering the energies and personalities of the human spirit or its relations with the world beyond the boundaries of sense.

Science also offers us data that can be helpful to us in our understanding of these areas. In my monthly seminar at Wisconsin Memorial Park called "Healing and Growing Through Grief," I ask participants to pay careful attention to what physicists are telling us today.

Energy does not die. Following the loss of a loved one, as grief begins to make itself felt, as our sorrow, pain, and doubts ask to be recognized, movement is required. Oftentimes, we run from grief. We suppress our heartache and then distract ourselves momentarily. We seek to minimize grief. Energy does not die. If we choose not to verbalize our feelings or share our thoughts and memories, or in some way do necessary and desirable grief work, grief will not disappear. It will simply come back and "eat us up." Countless numbers of studies have confirmed the catastrophic consequences of unresolved and delayed grief: physical disease, emotional disorders, automobile and household accidents, broken relationships, family crises and chaos, and low and impaired worker productivity. We need to be willing to recognize and work

with the energy within us and help to direct it outward. How is grief teaching us? What is it we are
learning from our grief?

When we look beyond death to life, of what value
is scientific inquiry? George W. Meek, in *After We Die,
What Then?* turns to science to support the theory that
for all practical purposes matter cannot be destroyed.

> It can only be changed from one form to another—that
> is, from one vibration frequency to another. This means
> that the law of conservation of energy applies to the
> energies of life as well as to material things.[4]

Meek finds these realities significant in looking for
evidence that the mind, personality and soul survive
the death of the physical body.

> The real you, your mind, personality and soul, is in a
> very real sense undetectable by our very limited five
> senses and this energy does not suddenly cease to exist
> just because the physical body which it has been wearing
> changes into water vapor and dust.[5]

Dr. Wernher von Braun, the eminent scientist who
helped create Germany's World War II rockets and
missiles and who later contributed greatly to the U.S.
space program, expressed the following thoughts
shortly before he died:

> Science has found that nothing can disappear without
> a trace. Nature does not know extinction. All it knows is

transformation! . . . Think about that for a moment. Once you do, your thoughts about life will never be the same.
. . . If God applies this fundamental principle to the most minute and insignificant parts of His creation—doesn't it make sense to assume that He applies it also to the masterpiece of His creation—the human soul? I think it does. And everything science has taught me—and continues to teach me—strengthens my belief in the continuity of our spiritual existence after death. Nothing disappears without a trace.[6]

I find it encouraging that in contemporary society, we have more and more testimony from the scientific community supporting survival in some form or other in some part of the universe.

Many people have had ESP experiences but are reluctant to share them. They fear ridicule and condemnation. The other side of this reticence is that many people exploit, sensationalize, or commercialize these parapsychological abilities and qualities. Justifiably, they receive a "bad press."

The following story gives us yet another sense of parapsychological experience. In 1760, the widow of the Dutch Ambassador in Stockholm was trying to locate her husband's receipt for an expensive silver service he had purchased and for which she was unfairly being charged. She approached Emanuel Swedenborg, known for his clairvoyant abilities, to

help her. A short time after, Swedenborg informed her
that he had seen her husband in the spirit world and
that she could expect to receive a message from him. A
few days later her husband communicated with her in
a dream, supposedly instructing her to go to the exact
place where she found the receipt she needed for proof
of purchase.

In *Beyond the Gates of Death,* Hans Schwarz cites the
biblical account (1 Sam. 28) of how King Saul, dreading his rival, David, and defying Israel's horror of the
occult, got a medium to conjure up for him the ghost
of Samuel, the prophet whom both kings relied upon.[7]

Another more recent example of clairvoyance often
referred to concerns the Rev. John Frederic Oberlin, a
Protestant pastor living in Alsace, France, for whom
Oberlin College in Ohio is named. "Oberlin claimed
that he communicated with his dead wife for seventeen years until she informed him that she had to
ascend to higher spheres."[8]

Recently I was in conversation with Carol, a sweet
and delightful friend of mine. Carol's husband, Arthur,
a deacon in his church, died most unexpectedly three
years ago. Both Carol and Art were deeply religious
people, dedicated to serving their church and spiritually sensitive.

Carol continues to be aware of Art's loving presence in her life, especially on various occasions during the last year. A couple of months ago, Carol's daughter lost an expensive gift certificate in the house. Everyone hunted throughout the house to find it, but to no avail. The next evening Carol turned to Art to ask for his assistance and was directed to the unused dumpster outside, where she found the gift certificate lying on the floor.

Episcopalian Bishop James Pike also reported having a number of these clairvoyant experiences following the suicidal death of his son in the sixties. These are reported in his book *The Other Side.*

Surely the human mind for some people may extend itself further into space and time than what the ordinary mind usually demonstrates.

The summer of 1980, my most beloved Aunt Bea died in Massachusetts. I had no intuitive awareness of her death, though we were very close. I was the great joy of her life, the daughter she never had. She was fully aware of my work in death, dying, and bereavement. Since her retirement, I had provided much spiritual guidance for her because she was open and responsive to this level of growth.

I returned east for her funeral and remained there a few weeks, receiving from her occasional signals after she made her transition. My first week back in Mil-

waukee, I suffered intense grief episodes, which
seemed to me well out of proportion. One evening I
thought, "I really don't understand all of this, and if
this feeling doesn't subside in a couple of weeks I'll
speak with a counselor." The next day, Sunday, I
attended church as usual. It was communion Sunday.
At one point during the service, when I returned from
receiving communion, I was deep in thanksgiving
when I felt my aunt's energy. I looked up and there she
appeared in all light and peace. I said, out loud, "O,
my God." She stayed for a moment, touched my spirit
lightly, and moved on. I never grieved again.

When we speak of telepathy, we often refer to
"reading someone's mind." It is more common than
we suspect.

Our dreams often carry messages to us. Not long
ago I counseled a woman whose son-in-law, a university professor, completed suicide. They had been very
close and shared similar sympathies in life. Eight
months after his death, he came to her in a dream and
instructed her to go to an unused computer in the
basement of his home. There she discovered a disc,
which had been stored away by him, containing his
very personal painful reflections and the circumstances
contributing to his decision to end his earthly life.

CHAPTER EIGHT

MYSTIC EXPERIENCES

Mystic visions and experiences are also considered to be non-ordinary states of consciousness. They are sometimes intense, overwhelming, and indescribable. We find them recorded throughout all historical periods and in every part of the globe.

Andrew Greeley, sociologist and director of the Center for the Study of American Pluralism at the National Opinion Research Center of the University of Chicago, writes that in American society today, mystic experiences are almost commonplace. "That almost two-thirds of the widows in the American population have had some contact with a dead person (presumably their spouses) is perhaps less surprising than the fact that two-fifths of the population who are not widowed also report such contact."[1]

What is reported again and again in these mystic experiences, and what seems to run through these accounts, are themes of overpowering joy, rebirth, penetrating light, peace, unity, bliss, and "a sensation of eternity"—the immediate, direct experience of a powerful spiritual force.

To illustrate this in a poignant manner, astronaut Edgar Mitchell described the impact of his February 1971 experience as he was returning to Earth from his Apollo 14 walk on the moon.

He affirms that when he went to the moon, he was as pragmatic a test pilot, engineer, and scientist as any of his colleagues, and he points out that many times his life had depended upon "the validity of scientific principles and the reliability of the technology built upon those principles." Nevertheless, during Apollo 14 he had an experience that contradicted his "pragmatic engineer" outlook.

It began with the breathtaking experience of seeing planet Earth floating in the vastness of space. The first thing that came to mind as I looked at Earth was its incredible beauty. Even the spectacular photographs do not do it justice. It was a majestic sight—a splendid blue and white jewel suspended against a velvet black sky. How peacefully, how harmoniously, how marvelously it seemed to fit into the evolutionary pattern by which the universe is maintained. In a peak experience, the presence of divinity became almost palpable and I knew that life in the universe was not just an accident based on random processes. This knowledge came to me directly—noetically. It was not a matter of discursive reasoning or logical abstraction, it was an experiential cognition. It was knowledge gained through private subjective awareness, but it was—and still is—every bit as real as the objective data upon which, say, the navigational program or the communications system were based. Clearly the universe had meaning and direction. It was not perceptible by the sensory organs, but it was there nevertheless—an unseen dimension behind the visible creation that gives it an intelligent design and that gives life purpose.[2]

Poets and artists likewise touch our hearts and souls with the fruits of their mystic experiences and revelations. Shakespeare, Milton, Wordsworth, Tennyson, Longfellow, Vaughan, Elizabeth Barrett Browning, and many others write with a profound understanding of our continuing existence. The subject of death and eternity, indeed, calls forth the genius of these creative souls.

"I saw eternity the other night, like a great ring of pure and endless light . . . calm as it was bright."

Henry Vaughan

"Heaven—the treasury of everlasting joy!"

William Shakespeare

Eye has not seen, nor ear heard, nor has it entered into
the heart of man those things which God has prepared for
those who love Him.

St. Paul, 1 Cor. 2:9

How do I love thee? Let me count the ways.
. . . I love thee with the breath, smiles, tears, of all my
life—and if God choose,
I shall but love thee better after death.

Elizabeth Barrett Browning

Marc Chagall is reported to have had a wondrous
vision while living in St. Petersburg. Drifting off to
sleep one night, he was awakened by the rustle of
wings. He witnessed brilliant light filling his room and
felt needles of pain lancing his forehead. Just then one
angel moved in the air above him. Gracefully and
majestically this elegant eternal visitor passed through
an opening in the ceiling, "carrying off with him the
light and blue air." Not long after that experience he
began painting "The Apparition."[3]

Father Andrew Greeley helps us to appreciate this
kind of extraordinary mystical experience in other
historical personages as well. In his book, *Death and
Beyond,* he cites the mystical way in which several great
spiritual leaders first experienced their call; the Bud-
dha, Jesus (at His baptism and at His transfiguration),
Paul (on the road to Damascus), Mohammed, and,

much later, Joan of Arc and Abraham Lincoln.

Father Greeley alludes to lifelong mystics, who often enter into trances, ranging from the shamans among the Amerindians and the dancers of Bali to the Spanish Carmelite John of the Cross.

Finally, he cites a few examples of how the mystics have suddenly perceived the triviality of what they had always taken most seriously: Thomas Aquinas's looking back on a lifetime of writing, G.K. Chesterton, contemplating a toy shop window, Paul Claudel, staring at a church pillar on Christmas Eve.[4]

All serious mystical traditions (Yoga, Zen, Jewish kabbala, Christian mysticism, the Gurdjieff "work") hold the belief that through dedicated commitment and training, ordinary human limitations can be transcended. Through this transcendence, reality may be perceived more accurately.

Through my own in-depth study of mysticism I was deepened, fashioned, and enlightened in my being and becoming, in my vocation and in my relationships. As I grew in my embrace and understanding and experience of Divine reality, I was tested in a multitude of ways in my ordinary human experience.

It was in 1967 following the death of Rudolph Morris that I began to experience after-death communication. A sociologist and teacher-scholar at

Marquette University, Dr. Morris was a profound man of God about whom the Jesuits said, "Here was a man touched in a very special way by the hand of God." He died at age seventy-three. The evening following his burial he manifested himself to me, bringing me peace and unity. Once or twice throughout the year I felt his presence in my classroom at the university, where I was teaching sociology.

The summer following his death, I had enrolled in a psychology of music course at the University of Wisconsin, Milwaukee. One day as I was about to enter Mitchell Hall for my afternoon class, I felt Rudolph's energy. As I looked up, I heard him say, "I must leave you now." I said, "I know." For the next five years I had no direct experience of Rudolph again, that I was aware of. From that time on, he has often been a part of my life. Rudolph has been helpful, supportive, and strengthening in my journey, offering wise counsel.

In 1970 I felt I was not growing enough in my relationship with God, so I elected to begin a fasting and meditation program on my own and a more active spiritual study. Simultaneously, I was teaching college full time. That year I chose to study several major works: *The Choice Is Always Ours,* edited by Dorothy Phillips, *Reverence for Life* by Albert Schweitzer, *God's*

Search for Man by Rabbi Abraham Heschel, *The Divine Milieu* by Pierre Teilhard de Chardin, and the Gospel of John. Over time I did experience new intimacy with Christ. I did come to know the presence and movement of the Holy Spirit with new sensitive awareness. I did experience more of the depth of myself and the mystery and fullness of God.

During the same time I suffered major losses. A close friend died just a day before Christmas. Three months later my grandfather died, three months after that my father died, and three months later a man I was planning to marry died. I tasted the depth of grief in ways I never believed possible. My pain introduced me to the depths of myself and drove me deep into the embrace of God.

I knew each of these deaths intuitively before I was notified or informed. In my grandfather's case, I was preparing to leave the house one morning to teach. As I reached for the door knob, I said out loud, "Somebody close to me just died." I sat on the couch trying to figure this out, but nothing more came. That evening when I returned home, I received a call from my youngest sister, Janice, living in Massachusetts, who said, "I have something sad to tell you, Grandpa died this morning."

Two months prior to my dad's death, while I was

in meditation, I was shown a prism turning, and the Lord said: "Your father is dying and I will take care of him." I communicated this in writing to his doctor, Jesse Baptista. Early one Sunday evening the day before my father died I was walking in the countryside when suddenly I fell to the ground on my knees. It felt as if someone had punched me in the stomach. After a few minutes when I stood up I felt fine, though I took it as a signal that something was in process that I did not understand.

Returning home and feeling "suddenly" extremely tired, I decided to rest, and as I did, I fell asleep. I had three dreams of my father . . . waking after each. In each dream, my father appeared and reminded me of all the fun we had enjoyed, and he thanked me for all we had shared together. (Dad was an active, committed elected political figure in Massachusetts) and I eagerly, joyfully worked along with him in my earlier days. In each dream, I said, "But Dad, we can't do that anymore." In the third dream, I took my hands and pushed him into the light.

When I awoke, utter calm surrounded me (though the dreams themselves were somewhat turbulent). I was drawn to the door of my bedroom where a white light streamed in. I had no lights on in the house.

I rose from bed and walked into the living room,

turned on a light, and reached for my Bible. I spent the next half hour reading from John's Gospel. I experienced the deepest peace. At 11 P.M. I returned to bed.

At 6 A.M. I arose and went to my office and then went on to do research in the basement of the college library. At noon I emerged. The librarian told me there had been a police officer looking for me earlier in the morning, so I walked over to the nearby station. As I entered, I said to the officer, "I'm Ms. Oliveira from the college and I understand you were looking for me." As he reached for a message on his desk, I uttered, "My father died last night, didn't he?" The officer said, "Yes, I'm so sorry. I see that they were able to contact you directly." Somewhat numbed I said, "No." He looked at me surprised and asked, "How did you know?" I said, "I just knew." He asked me if I knew what time my father died. I answered 9:30 P.M. My dad died at 9:28 P.M.

When I returned home, I received a telephone call from Dr. Baptista explaining the details. During the course of the previous year, my being so far from Massachusetts, the doctor and I had often spoken by phone. As he told me the details, he said that he really didn't expect my father's death to happen when it did. I reminded him of my letter. "Jacqui," he said, "I do remember your letter. You had a premonition, but I did not." We spent the remainder of our conversation recalling so many of my father's loving deeds, some which were familiar to me and some that were new. Dr. Jesse was a special and unique comfort to me that day, for which I am thankful to this minute.

I had no other experience of my dad during that time—at least not that I was aware of. My grief was profound. However, on Labor Day 1984, thirteen years following his death, I began to receive communication from him. From that day forward, I experienced his presence or helpful messages in various ways and at various times.

As I write this I am reminded of Marjorie, a wonderful woman, who many years ago was a member of my grief support group. Marjorie was a government employee and the mother of three adult children. One night she awakened in a cold sweat from a terrifying dream. She dreamed her thirty-five-year-old son was being dragged by a runaway horse. She awoke with the intense sound of stampeding horses.

Later that morning after she arrived at her office, she was about to phone her son. Just as she did, she received a call from Montana informing her that the sheriff found the body of her dead son. He had fallen from his horse and been dragged in the mountains. His skull had been crushed.

CHAPTER NINE

APPARITIONS AND MATERIALIZATIONS

Apparitions and materializations also feed our awareness of eternal life, the spirit world, and Divine activity. At a higher level, we have the presence of Mary, the mother of Jesus, in the world today. She seems to vibrate with a level of energy far beyond what we know on the human level.

She comes to awaken us to the love of God. She comes to help us realize how precious we are in the sight of God. She comes to activate Divine healing and spiritual awakening.

I am not a member of the Eastern Orthodox or Catholic Church. I do not write of Mary to promote any particular dogma. I have had a personal relationship with Mary for fourteen years. Mary doesn't belong only to the Catholic community or the Orthodox community, although surely these churches do the most for her institutionally. Mary is our Divine mother, our compassionate, universal mother. We know her effect at an individual level to be transforming.

In Mary's presence, hope is reborn, hurts are uncovered and healed. Mary invites us to open like a delicate flower before her, and, oh, how truly she cherishes our openness and vulnerability.

At a collective level she brings about conversion for many. Spiritual healings do occur. Faith in God, who authors and permits these visions and apparitions, is reborn. Her authentic apparitions have been reported from 1531 to the present.

Once again, geographically, collectively, and personally, we have the dimensions of space, time and matter transcended by the eternal. With it, new human purposes and directions unfold.

When we speak of materialization, we are referring to a person who has died and been buried or cremated reappearing in three-dimensional form in his or her entirety or just partially. The deceased physical body is instantly recognized. It is a rare phenomenon among lay people. Research in many countries has shown the recurrence of this phenomenon. During the last hundred years, small group research in international circles—Brazil, Germany, Poland, England, South Africa—has succeeded in producing materializations with the help in almost all areas of a medium.[1]

Reincarnation is accepted by more than half the world's population. In American society roughly thirty percent of adults profess belief in reincarnation even though it is strongly resisted in the Christian tradition.[2] The Buddhist Tibetan tradition embraces it. In Sogyal Rinpoche's masterful book *The Tibetan Book of Living and Dying,* we find clarity and inspiration related to reincarnation. Rinpoche's book is enormously popular in American society among readers of many traditions.

I applaud the death preparation work I find in the Buddhist tradition. Many are dedicated and deeply conscientious in their loyalty to the needs of the dying. However I do not support reincarnation. I see no need for it, given the growth possibilities and the grace of God available to each spirit person as his/her journey unfolds after death. Morton Kelsey, a psychological counselor and an Emeritus Professor, University of Notre Dame, writes in *Afterlife: The Other Side of Dying:*

> Life beyond death is neither a matter of successive reincarnations nor absorption into the absolute. It is rather the continuing development and growth of my own individuality in the presence of others like me, under the guidance of the Divine Lover. A kingdom or a banquet is a better symbol of this kind of life than a void. Workshop, love, learning and growth continue.[3]

I do believe, however, it is the prerogative of the Divine to permit reincarnation to fit Divine purposes. Whether or not a person adopts a reincarnation perspective does not dismiss the imperative that he must focus his energy in this life and develop as fully as possible. Tests will come his way and must be encountered in the present lifetime. Lessons of life must be learned and mastered in the here and now.

Serious scholarship and research have been done in the area of reincarnation by Dr. Ian Stevenson at the University of Virginia Medical School and by Dr. Karlis Osis, formerly the Director of Research for the American Society for Psychical Research. Those interested in this subject will find it helpful to consult their work.

There is increasing discussion today of mediumship and channeling. Mediums are of various kinds and subscribe to differing motivation and levels of feeling and quality. Generally speaking, a medium is a passive conduit through which messages flow from the other side.

Dr. LeShan draws a distinction between a *sensitive* and a *medium*. "The former," he says, "is a person who demonstrates precognition, telepathy, and/or clairvoyance with unusual frequency. A medium is a sensitive who explains her acquisition of information gained through the paranormal by saying that she gets it from "spirits" or "the souls of people who have already died."[4] Some have a native talent, and as with any talent, it must be used for the glory of God and the good of humankind. We must not ignore this talent or designate it as demonic. Reality and research demonstrate otherwise to many people.

Rosalind Heywood writes in *Beyond the Reach of Sense,* "The great medium is rarer than the great artist and we are fortunate if half a dozen crop up in a century."[5] But there are some, and they can and often do help searching souls to make sense of a loved one's death and achieve some peace.

For example, in the book *Our Children Forever,* Joel Martin and Patricia Romanowski tell of George Anderson, a medium of quality and talent. Working with children who have died to the earth and live on eternally, he delivers their messages to their bereaved parents. I often recommend this book to the bereaved parents I counsel, and I advise them to seek out other bereaved parents who have developed courage and fortitude while processing their tragedy and trauma. I often journey with them through their heartbreak, pain, and grief, and process it with them. I help guide their deepening faith in God, and I confront their doubts and resentments, confusions, and sense of betrayal. I also recommend the book *Five Cries of Grief*

by the Strommens. Both husband and wife write of
their individual experiences with and reflections on
their son's death from a spiritual perspective as well as
from a human one. I am aware that in the history of
mediums there has been enormous fraud. In addition,
some mediums are not accurate or particularly tal-
ented in carrying messages from the other side. They
may be adept, however, at reading the unconscious
desires of their clients and therefore be able to deceive
vulnerable clients. There is also a danger that mediums
might carry confused and garbled communication
because of interference from other intruding entities.
Some mediums are mercenary and exploitive. Some
try to manipulate God. Of course, it cannot be done.

Surely we must develop discernment. I believe we
can and must make good use of good mediumship.
Some mediums are of real quality and have real talent.
Some mediums are people of deep spiritual and
religious faith, people of prayer as well as psychic
talent. It is helpful to recognize this and cultivate the
talent and healing that these combinations bring.
However, even when we make good use of a medium
there is a danger of dependency on mediumship as a
means of assurance. Again, it is a question of personal
and professional integrity and balance on the part of
the medium and client. Again, the essential question is

one of faith and spiritual development. As you read and search, ask yourself if you want your commitment to be to developing the spiritual powers and faculties in your life and integrating these experiences and messages within your journey. Or do you want your journey to be defined only by psychic experience? If so, how does that fashion you for an ever real under-standing and commitment to the God of your Being, now and eternally? If so, how do you develop an authentic faith in the Divine for yourself? How do you become a more developed spiritual being?

I want to be very careful in discussing mediumship in a culture such as ours today. Spiritually, we are still a very underdeveloped culture. Psychic messages are no substitute for grief work. Psychic development is no substitute for deep spiritual growth or faith in God. Often, what happens today is that many people are seeking cheap spiritual tricks and sensational experi-ences. Often, we are confusing these experiences with in-depth spirituality and committed spiritual disci-plines and practices. In some ways we are a culture that is dependent more and more on the use of psychics and less and less on the demands and re-quirements of true spirituality.

Obviously, I find this tendency unfortunate. If one is to make true spiritual progress, one must try first—

with sincerity and humility—to open oneself to an honest search for God. Pursuing psychic abilities and experiences is often an obstacle to a full flowering of a spiritual consciousness rooted and centered in God. The more essential question, it seems to me, is, "How do the most significant questions of your life, your joys and sorrows, move you to nurture and choose to develop a relationship with the Divine and a desire for the fruit of the Spirit of God?" In what manner do you become more selfless rather than self-centered? In what way do you deepen your service to humanity? In what manner do you develop spiritual strength and live with integrity and higher purpose? In what way do you develop faith in the Divine and in the eternal?

I add here a note about channeling—a process growing in popularity today with certain audiences. Various kinds and degrees of this channeling can be distinguished as if on a continuum. At one extreme an independent spirit-personality from another level of consciousness embodies a human person and transmits information to a particular group gathered for the purpose of receiving the information. At the other end of the continuum, information is transmitted, but the source does not identify itself, and it is not identifiable.

Martin Israel, from long experience as a medical doctor and an Episcopalian priest, speaks of channeling in his book, *Life Eternal.* He sees the process of "channeling" as a mediumship in which a self-proclaimed authority lectures to a dedicated group of people about the afterlife, exhorting them to live meanwhile as virtuously as possible. The material published along these lines, though "intermediary" in character and lacking the uplifting inspiration of the classic mystical works, does sustain many who miss such nourishment in their places of worship. Such writings probably carry the germ of greater truths, as when they accept the survival of the personality for a fact without trying to prove it.

In his monumental coverage of this topic in his book *With Tongues of Men and Angels: A Study of Channeling,* Arthur Hastings writes:

> In my experience, there are few channels who provide counsel that is equal to that of an experienced therapist, an insightful and honest friend, a high quality psychic, or a specialist in the field. However, it is often possible to get a key insight, a new perspective, or critical information, because the process of channeling can reach outside the framework or set of the mind that has led to being stuck. It may provide stimulation which leads to creative solutions. It may have an integrative point of view or call attention to something overlooked. In all cases, the individual should be the one to decide how much weight to put on the channeled message.[6]

It seems to me that the search for meaning in our lives and the search for ultimate meaning do not begin or end in psychic experience. Viktor Frankl, for example, says that we find meaning in being responsible to the many calls which come to us from the particulars of our situation at any given time or place. This requires that we search, that we cultivate a relationship with the Divine, that we actualize self in the process, but that we transcend self. After-death communication and experience are not ends in themselves.

For some thirty years now, I have been receiving communications from those who have died to the Earth and moved on and who live and grow in eternity. I have learned, not without considerable caution and struggle, to be comfortable in and with the Spirit world. I never once asked for these experiences. They come, I believe, as gift and grace. They come at many levels, for many reasons, in various ways.

I am by profession an educator, sociologist, grief counselor, author, and spiritual teacher. I have for the last thirty years been dedicated to helping the bereaved. I have likewise been committed to spiritual healing. I have tried to be faithful to God's call on my life as I have understood it. I am by spiritual development a being in process and the result of many influences. I am a committed Christian.

I have not pursued the development of psychic abilities, though I am clairvoyant and clairaudient and I do relate telepathically. I have spent much of my energy seeking intimacy with God, cultivating and respecting human life as a faith journey. Because I am a Christian, I seek and find a life centered in Christ as most important to me. My life in Christ is inspired and guided by the Holy Spirit. Those of you from other religious traditions who are reading this book will find your own way to God, to the Divine, to this transcendent reality. As you seek to know and understand truth and respond to Divine reality, you will find fulfillment. You will make your own responses and find spiritual truth and your own knowledge and understanding of the Divine.

During these same thirty years, I have been fully immersed in working with the bereaved and the dying. The more I have traveled along these paths, the more frequently my after-death communication experiences occurred. I have learned to integrate these occurrences in my everyday life of work, play, love, and healing. I have also learned to integrate these in my teaching and counseling for the benefit of others. For each of us it is important to learn how to integrate the psychic and the spiritual and apply the benefits socially.

CHAPTER TEN

AFTER-DEATH COMMUNICATION

Ian Wilson, in early chapters of his *The After Death Experience: The Physics of the Non-Physical,* shows ancient people's accepting contact with the dead as natural, far more than we do today. He felt that the more a civilization developed, the more it lost of this faculty.[1]

Throughout my book I am trying to share various experiences of those spirit persons, ordinary ones and holy ones, who have died to the Earth and live on eternally. I am sharing experiences of after-death communication between spirit persons and those of us here on Earth.

The spiritual world is a communicative world. Those who precede us and are ready for the heavenly spheres, by the grace of God, communicate in various ways, for various reasons—some known and some unknown—and at various times.

Viktor Frankl, the eminent psychiatrist and, I believe, a profound man of God, teaches us from his own life and horrific experience at Auschwitz about the renewal that after-death experience makes possible. In his book *Man's Search for Meaning,* Dr. Frankl tells of once working in a trench. Outwardly, he saw just the prisoners, gray as the wintry dawn around them, but inwardly he was conversing with his wife, seeking a reason for his sufferings. Suddenly his spirit pierced that enveloping gloom, transcended that meaningless world and heard a victorious "yes" in answer to his search for an ultimate purpose. With the inward voice came an outward sign: in a farmhouse on the gray horizon, a bright lamp lit up and, as in the Prologue of John, "light shone in the darkness." There on the icy ground, amid the insults of the guard, he now felt his wife more present than ever, her hand within reach of his own. Then another sign: a bird flew down, perched on his freshly dug soil and looked steadily at him.[2]

Some of you have had after-death experiences of your very own. Perhaps you, too, have seen the spirit of your deceased partner at the foot of your bed upon awakening, or heard the spirit of your daughter call out your name while you were sewing. I received a call about five years ago from a friend. Ruth, a widow, is a retired high school art teacher; she is also a devout conservative Methodist. She told me that a year after her husband's death, one Sunday morning when she returned home from church, she saw her husband sitting in "his" chair waiting for her, looking at her with his usual smile. She was filled with an indescribable joy that remained with her for weeks. It was the one and only experience she had of the spirit of her dead husband.

Most people are reluctant to share their experiences with others—at least initially—so they maintain silence. They do not want to be criticized or appear suspect in the minds of others or feel foolish. They do not wish to be labeled crazy or hysterical. As Ruth was sharing her beautiful experience with me, she also confessed that she couldn't share it with most people she knew. "They wouldn't understand and would try to diminish it or talk me out of it," she told me.

Today there is more legitimate interest in the paranormal world, so with some gentle prodding, people often confide their very private, very beautiful, very real and lasting experiences to those who are competent enough to receive them.

Dr. Edie Devers writes in her book, *Goodbye Again:*

Experiences With Departed Loved Ones, of the correlation between after-death experiences and faith. In some cases faith is nourished and reawakened. In other cases faith is born for the first time.[3]

Dr. Devers tells of Anna, a sixty-six-year-old widow, who, while in the hospital, saw the appearance of her husband by her bedside. She reports him as being "solid" like any human person is. While Morey was with her, he kissed her and held her hand. His visit lessened Anna's worries about him and helped make her realize he was safe and happy. After his visit she gained strength herself and never became seriously sick again. Equally important, Anna became more serious about managing her own life, including her finances. She also expressed her gratitude to God for continuing to care for her husband. Anna believed "that Morey helped her to find God in a more personal way."

From that moment on peace deepened in her and she was able to commit herself more fully to her children and grandchildren. She knew in her heart the time would come later for her to join her husband.[4]

Whenever these experiences occur, they are always beneficent. They always bring peace. If you find an experience disruptive or frightening, you would be wise to reflect further.

Perhaps your negative reaction is due to an unconscious conflict within you, a combination of fears or projections, a chemical imbalance in your system, or medication that needs to be altered. Negative experiences may also be the result of spiritual warfare and demonic activity. If so, speaking to your pastor, rabbi, shaman, or spiritual advisor is essential if you are to claim spiritual victory, power, and authority in this experience.

After-death communication can take place through images, symbols, animals, thoughts, feelings, words, fragrances, touch, visions, the sense of a presence, and dreams.

Douglas, a forty-five-year-old widower who attended my monthly seminar, "Healing and Growing Through Grief," shared with me the following experience. About one month following the death of his beloved wife, Nancy, he and his daughter made a cemetery visit. While there, Douglas said to Nancy, "Send me a sign, please, to let me know that you are all right." He waited, listened, watched, and waited some more. There was no sign. His daughter then reminded her father they would be late for a meeting if they did not leave. Douglas took a few pictures of the gravesite before leaving to send on to friends and relatives. One week later when he received the photos, they showed a lovely rainbow over his wife's grave. This was not merely a sign, it was a significant sign, because during their marriage, each time the couple had achieved a new sense of unity and purpose in their marriage, a rainbow had appeared in the sky.

Another experience occurred about ten years ago when I met with Mary, the wife of a police officer who had been killed in the line of duty. Mary was very bitter, and she isolated herself for a good year. Finally, she was ready to begin grief work. As we worked together her life seemed to take on a little more meaning. When we were about to bring our eight-week session to a close, she told me that she was having strange experiences of her dead husband. "What might these be?" I asked.

She confessed that on occasion she would walk into a room and smell gardenias, which seemed to come from everywhere around her. Once she was immersed in this fragrance, memories would flow in rapid succession and she would hear the voice of her husband in her head giving her a message. No one else could smell these lovely gardenias. This happened not only in her hometown but also when she traveled out of town and out of the country. Experiences of this kind extended over a three-year period and were very influential in her own healing and the healing of others with whom she shared the information.

Dr. Louis E. LaGrand, in his book *After Death Com-munication: Final Farewells,* writes of an experience related to the loss of a sibling by a forty-year-old priest. His after-death communication came while he was making a spiritual retreat.

During his meditation time in the chapel he had a poignant experience of his departed brother, which helped him to realize that life continues after death.

> I looked up. It was as if the roof of the chapel opened up and I had an intense experience of my brother's face. I sensed his presence through the comforting smile of his face.[5]

As a result, this priest found himself more appre-ciative of others who confided their after-death experi-ences to him and more willing to engage with them. Prior to his experience with his brother, he was reluc-tant to do so.

Many of the people with whom I work, who have had similar experiences of this kind, deepen in their spiritual transformation and become more serious seekers of eternal truth, more compassionate and attentive to others who are following their own spiri-tual paths.

Bill and Judy Guggenheim write in their persua-sive book *Hello From Heaven* of a purchasing assistant for a university in Washington. Gary had experienced multiple losses—the death of his three-month-old daughter, Lauren, who died of sudden infant death syndrome (SIDS), his father, who died of a heart attack in his early forties, his grandmother, and his uncle.

Like those of others with whom I have worked who have reported internal visions of their departed loved ones, Gary's experience occurred while he was in his car and focused on his driving.

> All of a sudden, I had this image of my daughter sitting on my father's knee! He had one of his arms wrapped around her waist. Lauren was wearing a pink pinafore dress and was happy and smiling. Little Lauren was surrounded by other relatives in the spirit world. They were all peaceful and happy. Just before the vision ended, my dad said, "She's okay."[6]

This vision answered many of Gary's questions, strengthened his faith, and reassured him beyond measure. Young children do continue to grow and develop in the spirit world as they receive the nurture and love they need.

Six years ago I had a heartwarming experience involving one of my most treasured friends. Earlier in our lives, Doris and I had enjoyed many wonderful times together before she and her husband moved to Florida. The experience occurred in early December, while I was working the boutique at a performance of the *Nutcracker* ballet. As a member of the Friends of the Milwaukee Ballet, I have volunteered this duty each year for the last six years.

As I was arranging some of our merchandise, I was drawn to a special nutcracker ornament. The suggestion came to me, almost as a whisper, "I'm sure Doris would love to have that one." I paused for a moment, reflected almost in surprise, but then thought rather well of the idea. In fact, I realized I should have done so a few years earlier because it was Doris who had originally introduced me to the *Nutcracker* ballet.

The next day I mailed the nutcracker to her. Two days later I received a call from Harold, her husband, thanking me for the package that had arrived that morning. Harold said, "There's no way you could have known this, Jacqui, but sadly I must tell you that Doris died last week." I knew instantly the suggestion that I received at the boutique was from Doris, letting me know she had passed on.

I had two other experiences of Doris during the following month. One day while I was reading the morning newspaper, she came to me and asked, "Where is your birthday gift?" I was puzzled at first but after a few minutes walked over to my bookcase. There I found a book by Charles Swindoll entitled

Home: Where Life Makes Up Its Mind, which Doris had given me for my birthday in 1982. I opened it to the inside cover where, in her beautiful, flowing penmanship, I reread her message.

Dear Jacqui,

Each time we have shared our pleasurable adventures I have been warmed and filled to overflowing. I've experienced an affirmation that you believe in me and are willing to trust me. That is always so uplifting and inspirational for me.

May Our Lord's purpose and potential for you during the next year be supported and sustained by those of us who also believe in you and trust you wholeheartedly.

Fondly,

Doris

Sixteen years later, that message warms my heart, stirs my soul, and fills me to overflowing.

C. S. Lewis, out of the depth of his own life, offers grievers a penetrating and reassuring understanding of the grief experience in his book *A Grief Observed.* He also reflects on his after-death communication in very reasonable terms in the following selection.

I said, several notebooks ago, that even if I got what seemed like an assurance of His presence, I wouldn't believe it. Easier said than done. Even now, though, I won't treat anything of that sort as evidence. It's the quality of last night's experience—not what it proves but what it was—that makes it worth putting down. It was quite incredibly unemotional. Just the impression of her mind momentarily facing my own. Mind, not "soul" as we tend to think of soul. Certainly the reverse of what is called "soulful." Not at all like a rapturous reunion of lovers. Much more like getting a telephone call or a wire from her about some practical arrangement. No sense of joy or sorrow. No love even, in our ordinary sense. No un-love. I have never in any mood imagined the dead as being so—well, so businesslike. Yet there was an extreme and cheerful intimacy . . . it wouldn't be very like what people usually mean when they use such words as "spiritual" or "mystical" or "holy." It would, if I have had a glimpse, be—well, I'm almost scared at the adjectives I'd have to use. Brisk? cheerful? keen? alert? intense? wide awake? Above all, solid. Utterly reliable. Firm. There is no nonsense about the dead.[7]

Indeed, there is no nonsense about the dead—those who are alive in the spirit world beyond our own. Their love deepens and expands, their awareness and commitments increase.

Twenty-three years ago, my only brother, Michael, died at age twenty-eight. He suffered brain death and remained comatose for seventeen months before his body died along with his brain and he moved on. One month following his funeral, while I was experiencing deep grief, the space surrounding me filled with light, and the message I received was that I would hear from Michael again.

Naturally, I assumed that would be soon. The next day, I did not. The next week, I did not. The next month, I did not. Seven years passed before the only direct after-death experience I have had of Michael occurred. One day, after I had completed my morning scriptural meditation and was having no thought of Michael, I experienced him telling me that he now knew what his purposes were. He also told me that all I had shared with him while he was in coma had helped him to make his transition. At the time of his passing I had been 1800 miles away from him and communicated with him largely through prayer and meditation. At that time I was not feeling particularly knowledgeable or sophisticated in those spiritual disciplines. I simply thought through and talked out of my love for him and my faith in God. I knew deep in my heart that the Spirit of Christ would bring to completion whatever Michael needed most.

Not long ago I worked with a refreshing young woman whose mother had died. Kathy was a seeking soul. Her mother, a victim of cancer, demonstrated consistently to her family a passionate and firm Christian faith and deep soul wisdom in her living and in her dying. Most members of the family were in admiration of this mother and hoped to have the same kind of faith and development for themselves. The day she died, Kathy, her father, and her brother gathered around the mother's bed to receive her final blessing and share their love with her.

After, when they left the hospital, they took large helium balloons carrying loving messages to her and released them on the lakefront near the Milwaukee Art Museum. They then returned to their home in New Berlin, about twenty miles away. As Kathy took their dog out the back door, she found all three balloons wrapped around the tree in their back yard.

In these last few months I have received short messages from Bill Downey. His communication is always clear and direct. On one occasion, after a major undertaking in which I worked hard to reward many individuals, Bill asked me, "Do you know how to reward yourself now?" It had not occurred to me to consider doing so at that time, but Bill made me realize it was important.

Another time when I was struggling with a problem, he asked me, "What is your definition of courage?" I realized I needed to commit myself to a better sense and application of it. In both instances, I was freed and gained further insight and was able to use my own energy in more productive ways. Bill's communication has been, as C.S. Lewis writes, firm, keen, and utterly reliable.

Bernie Siegel, M.D., writes in *Love, Medicine and Miracles* that there isn't any obstacle to this intuitive, spiritual consciousness. It continues to unfold, and communication flows between those who have died and those alive on Earth. As Dr. Siegel has remained open to this, he has received many messages from his patients who have died.[8] I too have found that I receive correspondence from my grievers attesting to after-death communication.

I am reminded of a letter I received from Allison, a deeply intuitive, intelligent, and loving woman, twice widowed. Her first husband was killed in an automobile accident in England. Twenty years later, her second husband died in an airplane crash in Iowa. Allison writes:

> This past year has seen "growth" for me. Perhaps, it's more than some. It's hard to judge from day to day. Jim is a presence that is with me often and I can hear him clearly. I don't know why I couldn't feel him that first year—perhaps, too much shock and pain? I have lost the fear and anger, I think. And have gained some sense of security again. My own sense of self has reasserted itself. I feel I can go on living with some sort of positive expectation to the future.

Betty Ann, a very affectionate, warmhearted, and

humorous woman, the mother of four adult children, has been widowed four years. I received her letter a few weeks ago. She writes:

On June 5, Billie and I would have celebrated our fiftieth wedding anniversary. On that evening, our family gathered around me for a quiet "celebration"—actually, it wasn't so quiet. We had a very good time together and a very good time remembering their father. We wondered aloud if Billie knew that it was our anniversary. None of us had any sense of his presence there that night. However, the consensus was—surely he did, in his own way. This was Friday evening. On Sunday morning, I was moved to clean out a drawer. As I opened it, I was moved into the back of it and my hand closed around a small slip of paper—torn from a note pad. Lo and behold! It was a note Billie had written to me long, long ago. My finding the note confirmed for me that he is still watching over us.

Good Morning Darling,

I love you very much. Be a good girl today and think of me, now and then. Will call you later.

I love you

xxx's + a million

After I finished reading my husband's note, I reflected on the last line of the poem, "How Do I Love Thee?" by Elizabeth Barrett Browning: "...and if God choose, I shall but love thee better after death."

Carole, a most sincere, courageous, and compassionate woman and devoted mother and grandmother, has also been widowed four years. Recently, I received this correspondence from her:

> I want to share with you an experience I had last evening. I know you will understand and appreciate the deep meaning it has for me.
>
> When my husband, Rick, was alive, each year for fifteen years, we vacationed in Door County. While there eight years before Rick died, I bought him a wooden music box in the shape of a bell that played "Misty," his favorite song. Last night at 2:00 A.M., I was awakened from a deep sleep by the sound of that music box playing "Misty." I can't begin to tell you the depth of emotion I felt. I sensed Rick's presence as I made my way to the music box and it continued to play. I felt tears streaming down my face as I knelt to pray. Later I read passages from a book entitled *Count Your Blessings*. Once more, the meaning of our relationship and life together was confirmed. I believe God was allowing Rick to tell me that he is with me and continues to love me. I am so at peace.

In the spring of 1996, it seemed that I was experiencing many triggers to reactivate my grief over the loss of my father. As I approached the anniversary of his death, I was feeling somewhat forlorn realizing how much we had not been able to share. This was being amplified by many new events in my life that I knew he would have found as enriching as I did. I missed his charismatic ways, the fun he brought to so much of everything, and his enjoyment of me. I was struggling with this for the better part of a week.

At the same time, I was considering and reconsidering the direction my life was taking and my work commitments, and questioning the meaning of it all in light of other choices, opportunities, and pressures.

On a Thursday evening I was shopping for a birthday gift. As I waited for the clerk to complete my purchase, I was fingering books on the counter. I felt the prompting of the Holy Spirit as I picked up one of the books, and I was directed to focus and concentrate on it. As I looked closely I was stunned. It was a book written by Doug Sherman and William Hendricks entitled, in bold letters, *Your Work Matters to God.*[9] In small red letters at the top of the cover I read:

> From Washington to Wall Street to Main Street, work dominates the landscape of modern life. But unless you can connect what you do all day with what you think God wants you to be doing, you will never find ultimate meaning in either your work or your relationship with God. But how can you make such a connection?

When I turned the book over, the back cover was equally illuminating.

> Are you unclear on the value of secular work? What is

your view of everyday work? Are you pleased with your job, or do you suspect God would prefer you in some type of "full-time Christian service"? You need to come to some conclusion about this, because work is so central to life. [This book is a] demonstration of just how important secular work really is to God.

I thought, "How fascinating," and I laid the book down as the clerk gave me my change and my package. I left the store. As I was about to drive out of the parking lot, I heard the Holy Spirit say to me, "Jacqui, shouldn't you be reading that book?" I stopped and said to myself, "Maybe I should," but it was nearly 9 P.M., and I was tired and wanted to go home. I decided to return another day.

The next morning, I arrived five minutes before the store opened. When I finally entered I proceeded in the direction of the book I wanted to buy. Instead, I was turned in the opposite direction. After a few steps, I was face to face with a scroll hanging on a stand before me.

My Daughter:

I remember looking at you as a child, wondering what your future would hold. I wanted to shelter you from unhappiness and surround you only with wonderful things. I realize now that I could never have done this. For in order to appreciate happiness, you had to experience disappointment; to enjoy success you had to have

some failures; to feel true love, someone had to break
your heart. I couldn't protect you, but I want you to know
I was with you every step of the way. When I look at you
now and see the woman that has emerged from within, I
couldn't be more proud.

I stood almost transfixed, tears glistening in my
eyes. It was a communication from my father. I felt the
presence of his spirit to my right, and my spirit was
filled with love. As the clerk approached me (I was the
only other person in the store) she said, "Excuse me,
Madam, may I be of help to you?" I said, "No, thank
you very much. All of this just surprised me, but I
would like to purchase this." I left the store with two
gifts . . . new love and affirmation from my father and
new empowerment and guidance from the Holy Spirit.
This most resourceful book was one that I had been
awaiting for a very long time. Both experiences confirmed where I was and how I needed to proceed in
my journey. God's timing is always so trustworthy.

Not so long ago I had the opportunity to sit in with
one of our Family Service Counselors while he was
working with a family. While they were finalizing
paperwork related to the death of their grandmother, I
had a chance to dialogue with the son. Harold was a
business executive and the father of three adult sons.
He mentioned during our conversation that he had

been coming to Wisconsin Memorial Park regularly: once a month for eleven years, without fail, to visit at his father's crypt. I commented that he was indeed faithful. He went on to tell me that in each of his hour-long visits, he conversed with his father, experiencing his father's presence regularly and receiving many important messages from him related to his business and family life. This felt very natural to Harold—an extension of their life together on this Earth.

Both were of religious faith, and they had been professionals in the same firm. These visits were sacred to Harold. None of his siblings had ever had an after-death experience of their father at any time.

In the fall of 1976 I was teaching an afternoon college course called Understanding Death and Dying. One day on entering my classroom, I spontaneously decided we would meet in the cemetery for the next three weeks. I decided to teach my class at Rudolph Morris's gravesite. Because Dr. Morris had been responsible for introducing me to my college teaching career, I felt this site would be meaningful in itself.

During our second class together, my students were all very involved in doing process exercises following the delivery of an oral report. I sensed Rudolph's presence, and the message I received was that the girl I had just spoken with needed my help. I questioned the message and hesitated, since she was a very capable, vivacious student.

However, the next morning I called her into my office. I offered to help her with the dilemma she was facing, if she felt she wanted to share that. After a few minutes, she told me she was in an abusive relationship. We worked through many ramifications of this. As a result she found the courage to end the relationship and seek further growth and healing for herself.

In 1992 I was visiting with the thirteen-year-old son of a friend who had died about ten years earlier. This adolescent was rebellious and having serious difficulties. David, his father, had not been a strong personality, and while he lived on the Earth, not a very honest man. Upon meeting informally with Steven, surprisingly I received several successive messages from his father regarding honesty as the most important value in life.

In many of the after-death experiences I had with people who died earlier in my life, I recognized they had developed spiritually and changed. However, this was the first time I had received a message to pass on to another. I felt David's strength and love for his son as he relayed the message to me, and I was able to build further on that.

In some cases, those who pass on spend considerable energy trying to do repair work for those they love here on Earth. Sometimes we see this energy coming through in dreams in which they ask for forgiveness or leave a loving message that they did not communicate while they lived.

Again let me turn your attention to Patricia Treece's book *Messengers: After-Death Experiences of Saints and Mystics.* In it she recounts an incident in the life of Serada Devi, a Hindu saint, who had many after-death experiences involving her deceased spiritual leader and husband. On one occasion he came to comfort her because she was still prone to weep for him, and he said:

Why are you crying so much? Here I am. Where have I gone? It's just a change from one room to another—isn't that so?[10]

We find another precious example of after-death experience and faithfulness from the book *Hasidic Tales of the Holocaust* by Yaffa Eliach,[11] which Treece has retold in her book.

[T]he grand Rabbi of Bobov, Rabbi Ben-Zion Halberstam, had a special love for young people. Each Sabbath at the rabbi's house in the Ukraine many men and boys congregated to welcome the Lord's day with singing and dancing.

Then the Nazis arrived.

On July 25, 1941, the rabbi and his family were among two thousand Jews arrested. Four days later, the rabbi, dressed in his tall fur hat, was striding toward the open pits in the forest where the Nazis and Ukrainian collaborators were waiting to kill the entire group.

Urged to escape, the holy man said calmly, "One does not run away from the sounds of the Messiah's footsteps."

A short time later he was with God.

He was not a "survivor," but something greater: One who faces the worst that evil can devise and triumphs in spirit, entering the next life with the palm of victory.

Fourteen-year-old Moshe, one of those young boys who, in another world, had gathered at the rabbi's to worship God with joyous prayer and music, did not know of the rabbi's death as he himself—sole survivor of his large family—struggled to stay alive during the next four years as a slave laborer, first at Auschwitz and then, in 1944, at Mauthausen.[12]

Yaffe Eliach's account describes how Moshe felt certain that the rabbi continued to be present to him, offering guidance and protection in the midst of the intolerable pain, suffering, degradation, and brutality that define concentration camps. Moshe carried before him the vision of his dearly beloved rabbi as he remembered him often when he was a guest in the rabbi's home. Irrespective of the most extreme conditions of camp life, or the depths of his own despair, hunger, or physical suffering, Moshe could sense the rabbi ever so close to him. The rabbi would speak encouraging words that would empower him to go on living. His voice would comfort and soothe Moshe. Sometimes, he even felt the Bobover Rabbi directing his footsteps and leading him in directions other than those he planned for himself.

Treece continues:

> In prewar days, Moshe's favorite melody of the rabbi's songs was the one to which the rabbi chanted the holy Zohar, the mystical *Book of Splendor.* Any time life in the camps ground the teenager down to where his humanity began to slip away, he would concentrate on the rabbi's Zohar melody. Unfailingly this would produce "warm, human tears" that rekindled his spiritual fire.
>
> Then a bitterly cold winter decimated the ranks of the camp inmates through exposure, starvation, and disease. The growing fourteen-year-old was simply a bag of bones by December, 1944, when the prisoners were stripped of their filthy, thin clothes and sent into showers as part of a delousing regimen. Suddenly the naked men were ordered out on the parade ground, into what Eliach calls "a howling December wind." To reconcile a difference of one between the overseer's list and the number of actual bodies he had counted entering the showers, naked, starving men stood in this weather over an hour while

frost formed on their bodies. People collapsed and died. But the diabolical "count" continued.[13]

Eliach tells of how Moshe could feel himself becoming rigid and frozen, yet at the same time, extremely vulnerable and unsteady. Just then the Rabbi Bobov, Rabbi Ben-Zion Halberstam made his presence known and Moshe could feel the support he needed. He steadied Moshe and counseled him once again to sing and dance as it was his hope for survival.

Moshe could hear within himself the melody of the rabbi but he was too frozen to be able to sing. Then very slowly and painfully he felt his lips begin to move and heard the faint sound of melody begin to escape from them. Wondrously, his body also responded freeing first one foot so encased with frost, then the other crusted with ice. As Moshe looked down at the snow beneath his feet he realized he left drops of his blood and some of his skin from the sole of his foot there on the ice. Courageously, nonetheless, he began to dance in the snow to the rabbi's melody. Treece's account concludes:

When that period of horror was over, many lay dead on the ground. Young Moshe walked away.

Years later, a rabbi himself in Monsey, New York, when he told this story of the Bobov rabbi's care from beyond the death pit, Moshe's eyes glittered with tears.[14]

CHAPTER ELEVEN

EXPERIENCERS AND NON-EXPERIENCERS

I have often been asked by those with whom I work why they don't receive a message from a loved one who has died, when it's clear they so desperately want to do so. Why is it that one member of the family receives a sign and others do not, and why is it that a friend or neighbor receives a message and no member of the family does? These are sensitive questions asked by sincere, loving people. There are no definitive answers, but there is some hope.

It seems to me we must be open and flexible and often simply willing to rest with what doesn't make sense to us immediately. We must also learn to be discerning and wise. We must also learn to be content and appreciative of what is offered to us as a gift and not as a right or as a possession.

For many years of my life I had a few of these experiences, here and there, that I welcomed. However, I did not assign a purpose to them. In a sense, unconsciously, I let them teach me, prepare me. As I immersed myself more fully in my work, my experiences increased and I was able to understand the purpose and meaning of those experiences more fully.

Some people are uncomfortable trying to take any communication of this kind seriously or trying to understand after-death experience. Some people are simply too tense or too anxious and therefore not free and relaxed enough to receive communication. Some people simply are not interested. Others simply do not believe and never will believe in this realm of communication. Differences of this kind are to be respected. There is no obligation to make sense of signs and signals from the world beyond.

On the other hand, I can sometimes see in the people with whom I work and dialogue that after-death experiences come to them and they do not recognize or understand them.

This realm of after-death communication really belongs to Divine reality. We participate in it, we share in it, and we do try to understand it. Centuries have passed during which a great deal of experience, prayer, related literature, study, and research have occurred, yet we have not produced set patterns or absolute techniques for after-death communication. The mystery of God and eternal life, the spiritual world, is far too grand and beyond our conscious awareness for us to possess or understand completely.

Some of these after-death experiences happen spontaneously, some while a person is in crisis, and some in the midst of prayer and meditation. Some people long and pray for a sign and do not receive one. Some people do not pray and yet receive one.

I, myself, have never asked for experiences of this kind. They seem to come alongside the deepening of my spiritual development, the expansion of my be-reavement work, and the maturing of my love, wis-dom, humility, and compassion. I do not focus on them. I am genuinely humbled, and I am grateful to have them. Nevertheless, they do not substitute for the life work I am called to do here on Earth, the lessons I need to learn, the challenges I must meet. I, alone, am accountable for that.

However, I prefer to reframe the question I hear from my dearly loved students, clients, and friends. What is it that prevents us from recognizing after-death communication and what seems to foster it?

In general, I suspect that a multitude of fears, prejudices and ignorance learned from and reinforced by culture, religion, psychology, and family cloud our vision. Tension and inattentiveness also contribute their fair share.

It is true that our loved ones die. They are no longer available to us here, physically, concretely, or verbally in the way they once were. They will not come back to live with us here on the earth. It is very important not to deny death at any level. It is painful to delay grieving. However, it is equally true that our loved ones who died are living now as spirit persons, learning and growing at the next levels. It seems to me that we must recognize and respect this if we hope to take after-death communication and experience seriously and give this reality due respect.

We live within a vibratory energy system. We need to learn to recognize that this communication can and does take place through an energy exchange. Our loved ones are able to move energy to us and through us on occasion. Sometimes vibrations are received and felt within our own spirit.

Sometimes this is meant simply to make us aware that our loved one is remembering us. Sometimes this signals an incoming message in our mind or perhaps emphasizes one that has already been given. People commonly report to me feeling pressure on their shoulder, warmth in their hands, a tingling sensation in their face, or energy flowing through their neck. When this happens, I advise them to try to acknowledge the spirit person and to dialogue.

> Kevin, I feel your presence. Are you here with me? Is there something you want to say to me? Is there something I need to understand?

Then, be patient and comfortable with the silence and waiting period.

Sometimes a word, an image, or a question comes through, or a thought to ponder, that leads to further reflection. Sometimes a feeling of peace, joy, or tranquillity flows through you. Sometimes a loving memory is released that you had for a time forgotten. Sometimes you are led to a passage in a book or to find a document or address. Sometimes the right song plays nearby or you read a poem or a card confirming your relationship. Sometimes you find a gift symbolizing a decision you need to make or revealing the meaning of an experience. Sometimes this does not come right away but perhaps later that morning or the next day. Thank your loved ones. Tell them what you are aware of now and what you understand. Thank God for permitting this and let the experience go. Then move on to concentrate on your life, in the here and now, with a new gladness in your heart and a new reassurance in your spirit.

This is a learning experience. We learn to recognize
the energy of our loved ones and be responsive to their
signals and signs. We learn to be appreciative, if you
will—curious and expectant in a kind and positive
sense. We learn to listen. We need to listen patiently as
they concentrate their thought, and "speak," as they
share their energy, as they open us to new beauty and
their love.

Eternal spirits do draw near to us in goodness and
love, offering protection and helpfulness. They do not
linger. They do not remain. Often, before you go off to
sleep or when you awaken, your loved ones are near
to you and communication experiences of these kinds
occur. But our departed loved ones are aware of us at
many times throughout the day and night. We, in turn,
can send love and appreciation to them at many times,
as well.

In my own life, sometimes I think their thoughts,
feel their feelings. Sometimes I sense their presence
immediately. Sometimes I become aware of their
presence or a message only after an extended period
when I take the time to concentrate, reflect, and review
what has happened. Sometimes it happens after an
activity or a conversation I've had. I value the communication and experience offered me. I know how vital
and important it is.

Last summer I was speaking by phone with colleagues in Boston. It was only when I was writing them a follow-up memo, later that afternoon, that I was aware my father's spirit had relayed a helpful question through me during our conversation together. I smiled and I was encouraged.

Some people are very control-oriented, needing to program, plan, arrange details, and examine the parts of every happening. This surely cannot happen with after-death experience.

What are some of the other means that help us to open to legitimate experiences of this kind? Certainly prayer is an important and vital means of communication. For people of faith and devotion, prayer serves many beautiful purposes in their relationship with God. We can draw closer to God and include our loved ones by name and need in that intimacy. We can pray that they will grow richer in joy and deeper in love as they continue to discover more of themselves and more of the Divine. We can pray with them knowing they, too, continue to honor God and serve in ever new ways. Many pray to their departed loved ones for help and encouragement, and their prayers are answered.

On the first anniversary of Bill Downey's death I wrote a special commemorative service in honor of his new life in eternity. Early Friday morning the staff

gathered in the Chapel of the Flowers at Wisconsin
Memorial Park and together we prayed:

> Most loving and eternal God, we come before You this
> morning, humbly asking that you draw near and dear to
> each of us gathered here. By Your most precious Spirit,
> move each of us to a new openness and faith in Your love
> for us and in Your truth and reality.

> We come to You now in the spirit of friendship and
> faith, to celebrate the new life of William Downey as he
> continues to learn and move and grow in Your Heavenly
> Kingdom—in Your eternal Life and Love, Light and
> Peace. We pray for his progress, we pray for his creativity,
> we pray for his freedom from all limiting thoughts and
> feelings. We pray that he will continue to respond to all
> the love, happiness and spiritual gifts You have for him.

> We ask this in the name and in the power of Jesus
> Christ. Amen.

Meditation is another means of renewing and
receiving energy. There are various kinds of meditation—structured and unstructured. Each person must
discover what is most suitable and helpful for his or
her own growth and union with God. Meditation
alters brain wave patterns to the alpha state, in which
we are relaxed and yet awake. When this happens, the
nonlogical part of the mind becomes dominant, often
opening us to paranormal phenomena.

In meditating, we may, and often do, experience

after-death communication. Recently, during the month of April, I was taking some time for formal meditation. In one session I had an emotionally charged memory surface in me related to a deceptive and manipulative person. As I tried to enter it, Bill came to me with a question. "Is it possible that your colleague said that to punish you?" That had not occurred to me. Yet, it was exactly the catalyst I needed (and was resisting on my own) in order to understand a personality pattern that I had long denied. I seemed to reach a new level of freedom and empowerment because of this fresh awareness.

Another time I was struggling for a few days with family-related stress which was producing confusion and bewilderment within my being. While I was in meditation one afternoon in the fall of 1996, I had an experience with a spirit person who had died in 1985. Stella was a woman who loved me dearly in my adolescence and for whom I had great admiration and trust. She came to me in my meditation and said, very directly and firmly, "Mary was never ever honest with her husband." She then left. Immediately, all my stress seemed to dissolve. I could see the situation clearly, and I felt serene and at peace. I have not struggled with this matter again. I knew I had been given the right explanation and I could not be deceived again.

Serious mystics in all religious traditions are individuals who commit themselves to regular meditation practice, and they are changed intrinsically as a result. Their perception of reality, their participation in reality, and their sense of cosmic unity are shaped by their meditation process.

Meditation is a practice that cuts through religious and cultural barriers, transcends the dogma of religion, and helps establish a direct contact with the truth of one's being. In the afterword to *How to Meditate,* by Lawrence LeShan, Dr. Edgar N. Jackson says that meditation, "as the fusion of a disciplined mind and the creative spirit, is rooted in a compelling faith."[1] We must each ask ourselves how we use our minds, how we conceive of our spirits, and what value we assign to our religious/spiritual faith life as we seek ultimate meaning and experience more of it. Finding answers to those questions empowers us to come more fully into life and relationship with ourselves and the Divine. Ulrich Schaffer, in his book *Surprised by Light,* writes:

> I need time,
> uncluttered time,
> to center myself,
> to gather myself in.
>
> I want to find the center again
> that will keep my life together.

> I want to look into my own eyes,
> to become quiet
> in order to be able to love again.
>
> God offers himself as center,
> as axis around which all revolves,
> as the core of all things.
>
> He is the circle in which we are free,
> and in the circle the cross
> onto which we fall
> and from which we rise again
> to a life of love.[2]

Buddhist masters teach the essential practice of mindfulness, of bringing the scattered mind home, of bringing different aspects of our being into focus. They call this "peacefully remaining" or "calm abiding." Those in the Quaker tradition are encouraged to center deeply in the Light and grow in discernment and clearness through this meditative practice.

Recording our dreams and working with our dream images can be revealing and healing. I have helped many of my dear students and clients identify and take seriously after-death communication in dreams. Dreams can be interpreted at many levels. They can be a rich source of energy and insight for us. Often they bring new information and offer us clarification and assurance. Sometimes they stimulate ques-

tions that lead us to answers in our waking hours.
Sometimes dreams bring us face to face with realities
that we have not yet accepted. Sometimes we solve
problems in our dreams. All of this can be invaluable
as we develop our understanding and acceptance of
reality, life, death, and life beyond death.

Journaling freely and spontaneously is another
instrument of awareness and understanding. It is a
private discipline in which we can reveal ourselves
totally to ourselves. It can be clarifying for some: as we
think through what we want to say, we realize what
we are feeling. It can be a spiritual discipline in our
journey with God.

For me, journaling is central in my intimate relationship with God. It is also of major importance in my
experience with those I love here on Earth and those
who have died and live on now in Spirit.

I recommend journaling for many of my grievers.
It helps them to center in God more completely. It
helps many to understand their relationship with their
departed loved ones more fully. For many, new levels
of spiritual and psychological awareness expand.

Often I suggest a journal question, such as:

Eternal God, what is it you are asking of me now in my
life? What is it that you most value in me?

Sometimes, I ask people to complete a statement:

My life is changing now _____.

In order to keep people open to those who have died and live on now in Spirit, I suggest various statements and questions:

What I want you to know now is _____.

What I realize now since you died is _____.

What is it you want me to know, to understand, to accept now? _____.

Body work, breathing exercises, Yoga, stretching, and massage therapy can also help us to keep our energy channels open.

Overall, it's important to value and cultivate our intuitive faculties. This does not mean we should neglect critical thinking or reduce the importance of our rational mind. The intuitive perception of reality includes extrasensory perception, telepathy, clairvoyance, clairaudience, artistic inspiration, and mystical religious experience.

During the last twenty years, brain research has given us much information about the two hemispheres of the brain. The left hemisphere is predominantly verbal, rational, and linear in its functioning. The right is predominantly intuitive and holistic. Opening up our intuitive faculties through education and training can give us a wider range of choices, possibilities, and freedom. Intuitive experiences expand consciousness.

We come to know more of reality and truth.

The role of intuition is to lead us into what is new, beyond what is familiar and known to us, and it helps us make discoveries. Intuition can operate at a personal level, in everyday life as we think, feel, observe, and participate in ongoing activity and reality. It can operate also on a transpersonal level, when we focus on the Life of the Spirit, Divine Truth, Divine Life, and Divine Love. Intuitive experience at this level engages us at the highest levels with Spiritual Wisdom, Love, Peace, and Joy, and causes us to deepen our appreciation of the Divine.

Intuition is not opposed to reason, but works with it to complement it. Physicist Fritjof Capra says:

> Rational knowledge and rational activities, though all-important, are not the whole of scientific research. They also call for the intuition that leads to the creative insights that come so suddenly at moments of disengagement from intellectual effort and that lend joy to the scientist's research.[3]

After much intellectual inquiry and logical pursuit of a subject, I often become, as most people do, somewhat numb, exhausted, and unable to go further. Later, when I am not expecting it, many insights intuitively start to come to me, and I am able to move once again.

CHAPTER TWELVE

DISCERNMENT

U ndoubtedly, there will always be a struggle
between the rationalists—the thinkers who
seek and discover God primarily through
reasoning, analysis, reflection, and the word—and the
mystics who see God more easily in contemplation,
signs, images, symbols, visions, and wonders.

A rationalistic framework has been dominant in
the western world. It is in need of perceptual, intuitive
knowledge if our hearts are to remain open to the
wonder and grandeur of God and ourselves as spiritual beings.

Our full development as human persons calls for
the exercise of both our thinking and feeling faculties. I
would like to believe we are making some better
progress today calling forth and respecting both
perspectives.

Every major religion has both the rationalists and the mystics. Every church, synagogue, mosque, and congregation has both. Both are necessary for the full revelation and appreciation of God. The presence of God cannot be manipulated or controlled by any of us. It can only be experienced by us as we search and respond. It is made possible by the graciousness and beauty of a trustworthy, loving God who desires to be known by each of us.

Especially in our western spiritual belief systems, most major religions—at least institutionally—have maintained ambivalence with the spirit world. Among fundamentalists and extreme conservative groups, there is outright condemnation. No person is to summon up or entertain the spirits and thus tempt demons and open himself or herself to their influence. Among other religious groups, experiences that occur spontaneously or are initiated by those on the other side are more easily tolerated and accepted.

I completely agree that we must be discerning in our contact and communication with the spirits and in the understanding we have of God's world beyond our own.

About four years ago, while Bill was alive on Earth, he asked me to consider offering a seminar for the public on angels as part of our monthly program-

ming at Wisconsin Memorial Park. Bill felt this would
be helpful for people interested in spiritual growth.

I agreed. It has been an enormously popular
seminar, attracting some 200 people twice a year.
Those who attend this seminar agree it is spiritually
nourishing for them.

In that seminar, I treat the beauty and majesty of
God's angels and the wonder and increase of angelic
activity in the lives of people in our contemporary
world. I cover the unpopular notion of evil and demonic activity present in our lives and world today
that are operating in our thinking and behavior. I also
speak of the meaning and development of discernment
in our lives.

These topics are of vital concern to each of us in
our spiritual development, in our life as we live it in
this world, and in our relationship with the Divine.

The term "discernment" refers to a sense of cutting,
separating, sifting through. In ordinary conversation
when we refer to someone who has discerning taste
we mean he or she has refined taste, able to recognize
differences in quality, both apparent and subtle.

"Discernment stresses skill and accuracy . . . a
capacity for distinguishing and selecting the excellent,
the appropriate, or the true. . . . Perception implies
quick, acute discernment and delicacy of feeling."[1]

Spiritually, discernment means an increasing awareness of the presence of God in all that we say, do, think, feel, and have. Discernment refers to the expanding awareness and embrace of Divine truth and freedom as we develop and learn to use our reason, emotions, imagination, and will.

Discerning the spirits involves a process of enlightenment, a struggle to see what is of God for us, what is not of God for us—what comes from the forces of Light, what comes from the power of darkness within us and around us. This calls for faithfulness and integrity and wisdom on our parts, which is a daily process in seeking and reflecting the light of truth.

Daily experience teaches us this well: that we must fight off evil impulses within us, so that greater impulses will emerge. Daily, we must learn to identify errors in our thinking and judgment so that increasingly we will become beacons of light and bearers of truth.

We live in a culture, a world, I believe, that takes evil far too casually. We compromise, we tolerate, we ignore evil, instead of confronting, exposing, challenging, and overcoming it.

Gary Zukav, writing in *The Seat of the Soul,* says that evil is an absence of light, love, and completeness.[2]

Evil thoughts and spirits bind us, keep us isolated,

keep us locked in a state of inferiority, shame, defeat, oppression, greed, fear, hopelessness, and mockery. Evil locks us in cynicism, negativity, self-destruction, addiction, deception, degradation, and blindness. Demonic activity causes dissipation of energy and stirs up corruption, confusion, and chaos within our souls, within our minds, and in our feelings, our relationships, and our world.

American psychiatrist M. Scott Peck writes, in his groundbreaking book *People of the Lie:*

> The evil deny the suffering of their guilt—the painful awareness of their sin, inadequacy, and imperfection—by casting their pain onto others through projecting and scapegoating. They themselves may not suffer, but those around them do. They cause suffering. The evil create, for those under their dominion, a miniature, sick society.[3]

On the other hand, the more we take seriously ourselves as children of God, and the more we desire to live in communion with God, here and eternally, the more we will hunger and thirst for Divine life within us and in our world, and the more we will choose a life of wisdom, love, compassion, humility, and clarity over narcissism (the need to be worshipped), domination (the need to be superior), and manipulation (the need to control circumstances and others to fit our own demands and agenda).

This development requires that we center into the God of our being, that we be ever watchful and attentive to the ways and movement of the Spirit in us and in our lives. This is no elementary task in a world that clamors hourly to win us over with distractions too numerous to mention. It requires that we be discerning, that we decide in the best ways possible to develop in the best ways possible. It requires that we value and recognize the confirmation of the Spirit of God in our lives.

We are called to overcome evil with good. We are called to claim our divine heritage and reflect the power and will of God in this life. The Holy Spirit of God empowers us in this process now and throughout our eternal journey. Just as we come to know the Holy Spirit here in our earthly journey, so too are we led and guided in the heavenly spheres by the presence and Spirit of God in our continuing unfoldment.

The after-death communication and experience I have shared with you has brought deeper faith, hope, and love to those involved. It has helped those loving people to deepen their commitment to God and their awareness of themselves as children of God. It has promoted new and greater reverence for and service to family and community. It has enriched their church fellowship and contributed to healing and greater understanding of the human journey and the eternal journey for themselves and others. It has in no way diminished the Divine or interfered with the demands and meaning of faith or grace. It has not lessened the capacity of the people in this book to celebrate the gift of life. Rather it has enlarged and validated it.

"The psychic mode used by people with intelligence and spiritual discernment," says the Episcopalian priest Martin Israel, M.D., "is one of intimate communication between people and between the Divine and the human. It is sad that it has been sensationalized, cheapened, and brought under ridicule in a materialistic society and in a spiritualistic sense."[4]

In the past forty years, we have moved, it seems to me, from ignorance and ambivalence and overwhelming fear in the areas of death and dying, bereavement, and after-death communication to a more reliable knowledge, understanding, and experience of these realities.

That movement has been slow and cautious, but it has been for some of us positive, steady, and conscientious. Science, psychology, sociology, and theology have made and are making meaningful contributions in these sensitive areas. Alone they are insufficient. We live and move and have our being and becoming in the midst of manifold mysteries. Poetry, mysticism, spirituality, parapsychology and experience with the dying person, personal religious faith, and experiences with spirit persons who have preceded us in death and live in worlds beyond—all of these can and do help to enlighten and educate us, leading us to deeper transformation, revelation, and faith. As a result, new confidence, faith, understanding, and healing can occur. Love is eternal and so is life for each one of us.

Divine revelation has always come to us here on Earth in many ways. It remains for those of us with discerning minds and hearts to treat as holy our direct experience with the dying and those who have completed their human lives and live on now in Spirit. It remains for us to integrate the meaning of these experiences in our daily lives, our own spiritual journey, and faith life.

God does not permit us to have spiritual experiences so that we keep them hidden. They must be offered for the inspiration and confirmation of all in the human family who are ready and able to receive them and use them wisely. The experiences I, for one, have had during these last thirty years have been consistent, and filled with grace.

I am more intimate with God, more centered in Christ, more sensitive to the Holy Spirit, more authentic and committed to my Christian faith, and more engaged in human life and healing because of all of them. Psychologically I am more whole, more truly the woman I am called to be. Emotionally I am more stable and more flexible. Spiritually I am more rather than less vigilant, more rather than less perceptive.

Rev. Canon William V. Rauscher served in the Episcopal ministry for forty years and in one parish alone for thirty-six years. He was once president of an organization known as Spiritual Frontiers Fellowship. In addition to his parish ministry he spent decades exploring psychic phenomena. In his book, *The Spiritual Frontier,* he points out the difference between the mystical and psychical. Spiritual experience is viewed from a religious perspective while parapsychology can be purely secular. Although hard to prove and with various interpretations, a spiritual experience can deepen our understanding of God and our relationship to the Divine.

Parapsychology, on the one hand, attempts to prove in the laboratory, in a controlled environment, what can seldom be proved on a personal experiential level. For example, parapsychology does help us with questions of precognition that challenge our concepts of past, present, and future, questions of telepathy and clairvoyance that challenge our concept of space, and other questions dealing with the mysteries of the afterlife. On the other hand, a commitment to life as a faith journey helps us to discover and rediscover a Divine Thinker-Artist-Architect-Musician, ever at work to make up for the sorrows and injustices of our lives, and of this human world.

Through these insights, we come to understand that everything has a purpose, so that no tear is wasted, no cup of water given in vain, but all is part of one great whole, one final homecoming. Rauscher adds, "And the name of all this wonder is God, whom Jesus taught us to call Father."[5]

Throughout my book I have tried to offer you knowledge, and clarification, for your own search and journey. I have tried to awaken you to the loving, empowering effects of after-death communication and experience permitted by God.

After we die, each of us continues to unfold in Spirit as individuals. We deepen and expand our thought patterns. We praise and adore in the heavenly realms. We grow in love and forgiveness. Our creative gifts and talents multiply. We are capable of movement and discovery in God's eternal universe.

The grace of God is eternally offered to us. We must respond. Purification and reparation are part of our new life to ensure even greater life. Reunion with those we love and who love us is real. They continue to love us. They try to help us. We need to recognize and appreciate that experience when it comes, and be nourished because of it. We need, then, to release it to God and continue on with our own gladness and a seasoned faith.

Alan Jones writes that to feel banished and alienated, and to yearn to be welcomed home again, represent the cry of contemporary men and women. He points out that Carl Jung often wrote of the poverty of modern spirituality, which lacks a sense of wholeness and vision. We diminish our humanity when we deny or become indifferent to our spiritual depths.[6]

Dr. Bruce Larson, sometimes referred to as the founder of relational psychology, reminds us in his book *The Presence: The God Who Delivers and Guides* that a relationship of love is a relationship of trust. God has a deep desire for intimacy with each and every one of us, wants to trust us, wants to receive our trust in return. "There is only one place of true lasting security and that is in God," says Dr. Larson. "It is a privilege to be ever moving on our journey at God's invitation both here and eternally."[7] This journey offers us many discoveries and requires authentic response from us.

Teilhard de Chardin, writing in *The Divine Milieu,* says, "that we must overcome death by finding God." "Eternal life," as Dr. Leslie Weatherhead says, "is to be thought of as quality and not quantity, not in endless years but in a quality of communion with God which clearly begins now."[8]

I teach my dearly loved students that each of us, individually, will continue by the grace of God to develop and ascend with joy as we recognize and respond to the life and love God offers us here on this good Earth and in the wondrous world beyond.

> For with You is the fountain of Life
> In Your light we see light. (Ps. 36:9)

NOTES

PREFACE

1. Mitch Albom. *tuesdays with Morrie.* (New York: Bantam Doubleday, 1997), p. 80.

CHAPTER ONE: FINDING MEANING IN DEATH EXPERIENCES

1. Sidney Piburn (ed). *The Dalai Lama: A Policy of Kindness.* (Ithaca: Snow Lion Publications, 1993), p. 96.
2. Glen Davidson. *Living With Dying.* (Minneapolis: Augsburg Publishing, 1975), pp. 17–21.
3. Sogyal Rinpoche. *The Tibetan Book of Living and Dying.* (San Francisco: Harper, 1993), pp. 7–8.
4. Daniel C. Maguire. *Death by Choice.* (Garden City: Image Books, 1984), p. 1.
5. Lucinda Vardey, ed. *God in All Worlds.* (New York: Vintage Books, 1995), p. 545.
6. "Death," in 1998 *Grolier Multimedia Encyclopedia* (electronic media), by Grolier Interactive, 1997.

CHAPTER TWO: EGO GROWTH AND SOUL GROWTH

1. Norman Vincent Peale. *The Healing of Sorrow.* (Norwalk CT: C. R. Gibson Co. 1966), p. 16.
2. Dorothy J. Hulst. *As a Woman Thinketh.* (California: DeVorss & Co., 1910), p. 64.
3. Carl Sagan. "In The Valley of the Shadow," in *Parade Magazine* (March 10, 1996), pp. 18–21.
4. Bob and Elizabeth Dole. *The Doles: Unlimited Partners.* (New York: Simon & Schuster, 1988), p. 215.
5. 2 Cor. 12:2–4.
6. Rose Ann Bradley. "A Child's View of Heaven," in *Marriage and Family Living.* (August 1987), pp. 17–18.
7. Bernard Gittelson. *Intangible Evidence.* (New York: Simon & Schuster, 1987), pp. 23, 27.

CHAPTER THREE: NEAR-DEATH EXPERIENCES

1. Raymond Moody. *The Light Beyond.* (New York: Bantam, 1998), p. 194.
2. George Gallup and W. Proctor. *Adventures in Immortality: A Look Beyond the Threshold of Death.* (New York: McGraw-Hill, 1982), p. 6.
3. Hans Schwarz. *Beyond the Gates of Death: A Biblical Examination of Evidence For Life After Death.* (Minneapolis: Augsburg Publishing, 1981), pp. 40–41.
4. Melvin Morse. *Parting Visions.* (New York: Villard Books, 1994), p. 77.
5. Phillip L. Berman. *The Journey Home: What Near-Death Experiences and Mysticism Teach Us About the Gift of Life.* (New York: Simon & Schuster, 1996), p. 34.
6. Ibid., p. 36.

CHAPTER FOUR: OUR SECOND BODY

1. Elisabeth Kübler-Ross. *On Life After Death.* (Berkeley: Celestial Arts, 1991), pp. 49–50.
2. Sig Synnestvedt. *The Essential Swedenborg.* (New York: Twayne, 1970), p. 106.
3. Patricia Treece. *Messengers: After-Death Appearances of Saints and Mystics.* (Huntington, IN: Our Sunday Visitor, 1995), p. 38.
4. Herbert Weiner. *9½ Mystics: The Kabbala Today.* (New York: Macmillan, 1992), p. 48.
5. Ibid.

CHAPTER FIVE: LIFE REVIEW

1. David Lorrimer. "Near Death Experiences and Ethical Transformation," *Noetic Science Review.* (Winter 1994), p. 39. From a talk given at the Institute of Noetic Sciences conference "The Sacred Source: Life, Death, and the Survival of Consciousness," Chicago, July 15–17, 1994.
2. Martin Buber. *Tales of the Hasidim.* (New York: Schocken Books, 1991), p. 311.

3. Alexander Cruden. *Cruden's Complete Concordance of the Old and New Testament.* (Grand Rapids: Zondervan Publishing House, 1967), pp. 210–11.
4. Martin Buber. *A Believing Humanism: My Testament, 1902–1965.* (New York: Simon & Schuster, 1967), p. 231.
5. Ephraim Llewellyn Eaton, D.D. *Our Friends Immortal: Can We Talk With Them?* (Milwaukee: Advocate, 1946), p. 62.
6. Ibid, pp. 62–63.
7. Carroll E. Simcox. *The Eternal You: An Exploration of a Spiritual Intuition.* (New York: Crossroad, 1986), p. 44.
8. Mary Baker Eddy. *Science and Health With Key to the Scriptures.* (Boston: First Church of Christ, Scientist, 1875), p. 3.
9. Phillip Keller. *The Inspirational Writings of Phillip Keller. A Shepherd Looks at the Good Shepherd and His Sheep.* (New York: Inspirational Press, 1993), p. 412.
10. Simcox, p. 4.
11. Leslie Weatherhead. *Life Begins at Death.* (Nashville: Abingdon Press, 1969), pp. 31–32.

CHAPTER SIX: DEATHBED VISIONS AND TRANSITIONS

1. John Myers. *Voices from the Edge of Eternity.* (Uhrichsville, OH: Barbour & Co., 1968), p. 162.
2. Ibid., p. 59.
3. Ibid., pp. 46–47.
4. Ibid., p. 79.
5. Billy Graham. *Angels: God's Secret Agents.* (Garden City, NY: Doubleday & Co, 1975), p. 152.
6. Carol Nieman and Emily Goldman. *Afterlife.* (New York: Viking Books, 1994), p. 218.
7. *John Wesley's Little Instruction Book: A Classic Treasury of Timeless Wisdom and Reflection.* (Tulsa: Honor Books, Inc., 1997), p. 155.
8. Anne Wallace Sharp and Susan Handle Terbay. *Gifts: Two Hospice Professionals Reveal Messages From Those Passing On.* (Far Hills N.J. : New Horizon Press, 1967), pp. 17–19.
9. Leslie Weatherhead. *Life Begins at Death.* (Nashville: Abingdon Press, 1969), p. 17.

10. Ibid., p. 17.
11. Ram Dass. *Grist for the Mill.* (Berkeley: Celestial Arts, 1988), p. 116.
12. Melvin Morse. *Parting Visions.* (New York : Villard Books, 1994), xii.

CHAPTER SEVEN: EXTRASENSORY PERCEPTION

1. J. B. Rhine. "Reality of the Spirit," *Guideposts.* September 1963, pp. 10–11.
2. Lawrence LeShan. *The Medium, the Mystic and the Physicist: Toward a General Theory of the Paranormal.* (New York: Viking, 1974), pp. 65–66.
3. Carroll E. Simcox. *The Eternal You: An Exploration of a Spiritual Intuition.* (New York: Crossroad, 1986), p. 6.
4. George W. Meek. *After We Die, What Then?* (Columbus, OH: Ariel Press, 1987), pp. 78–79.
5. Ibid., p. 79.
6. Ibid.
7. Hans Schwarz. *Beyond the Gates of Death: A Biblical Examination for Life After Death.* (Minneapolis: Augsburg Publishing, 1981), p. 58.
8. Ibid., p. 57.

CHAPTER EIGHT: MYSTIC EXPERIENCES

1. Andrew Greeley. "Correlates of Belief in Life After Death." *Sociology Social Research* 71. (July 1987): 3–8.
2. Willis Harman and Howard Rheingold. *Higher Creativity: Liberating the Unconscious for Breakthrough Insights.* (New York: Putnam, 1984), pp. 155–56.
3. Thomas Fleming. "Marc Chagall's Angelic Inspiration." *Guideposts,* July–August 1998, p. 41.
4. Andrew Greeley. *Death and Beyond.* (Chicago: Thomas More, 1976), p. 91.

CHAPTER NINE: APPARITIONS AND MATERIALIZATIONS

1. George W. Meek. *After We Die. What Then?* (Columbus, OH: Ariel Press, 1987), p. 63.

2. Richard N. Ostling. "The Church Search." *Time* 5. (April 1993): 44–48.
3. Morton Kelsey. *Afterlife: The Other Side of Dying.* (New York: Paulist Press, 1979), inside cover.
4. Lawrence LeShan. *The Medium, the Mystic, and the Physicist: Toward a General Theory of the Paranormal.* (New York: Viking, 1974), xii.
5. Rosalind Heywood. *Beyond the Reach of Sense.* (New York: E. P. Dutton & Co., 1961), p. 54.
6. Arthur Hastings. *With the Tongues of Men and Angels: A Study of Channeling.* (Ft. Worth: Holt, Rinehart & Winston, 1991), p. 34.

CHAPTER TEN: AFTER-DEATH COMMUNICATION

1. Ian Wilson. *The After Death Experience: The Physics of the Non-Physical.* (New York: William Morrow, 1987), pp. 15, 17–26. (See especially Chapter 2, "In Touch with the Departed.")
2. Viktor Frankl. *Man's Search for Meaning.* (New York: Pocket Books, 1984), pp. 60–61.
3. Edie Devers. *Goodbye Again: Experiences with Departed Loved Ones.* (Kansas City: Andrews & McMeel, 1997), p. 149.
4. Ibid., pp. 147–49.
5. Louis LaGrand. *After-Death Communication: Final Farewells.* (St. Paul: Llewellyn Publishers, 1997), p. 51.
6. Bill Guggenheim and Judy Guggenheim. *Hello From Heaven.* (New York: Bantam, 1996), p. 109.
7. C. S. Lewis. *A Grief Observed.* (New York: HarperCollins, 1961), p. 59.
8. Bernie Siegel. *Love, Medicine and Miracles.* (New York: Harper & Row, 1986), p. 220.
9. Doug Sherman and William Hendricks. *Your Work Matters to God.* (Colorado Springs: NavPress, 1987).
10. Patricia Treece. *Messengers: After Death-Appearances of Saints and Mystics.* (Huntington, IN: Our Sunday Visitor, 1995), p. 315.
11. Ibid, pp. 307–308. Quoting Yaffa Eliach. *Hasidic Tales of the*

Holocaust. (New York: Oxford University Press, 1982), pp. 184–87.
12. Eliach, ibid., p. 185, quoted by Treece, ibid., p. 307.
13. Eliach, ibid., p. 186, quoted by Treece, ibid., p. 308.
14. Eliach, ibid., p. 187, quoted by Treece, ibid.

CHAPTER ELEVEN: EXPERIENCERS AND NON-EXPERIENCERS
1. Lawrence LeShan. *How to Meditate.* (New York: Bantam-Doubleday, 1975), p. 152.
2. Ulrich Schaffer. *Surprised by Light.* (New York: Harper & Row, 1980), p. 14.
3. Fritjof Capra. *The Tao of Physics.* (Berkeley: Shambala, 1975), p. 31.

CHAPTER TWELVE: DISCERNMENT
1. *Webster's New Collegiate Dictionary.* (1973)
2. Gary Zukav. *The Seat of the Soul.* (New York: Simon & Schuster, 1989), p. 69.
3. M. Scott Peck. *People of the Lie.* (New York: Simon & Schuster, 1983), p. 305.
4. Martin Israel, M.D. *The Dark Face of Reality.* (New York: HarperCollins, 1989), p. 100.
5. William Rauscher. *The Spiritual Frontier.* (New York: Doubleday, 1975), p. 178.
6. Alan Jones. *The Soul's Journey: Exploring the Three Passages of the Spiritual Life with Dante as a Guide.* (San Francisco: Harper & Row, 1995), p. 5.
7. Bruce Larson, Ph.D. "The Presence: The God Who Delivers and Guides." Part I Videotape, *Hour of Power,* Crystal Cathedral, Garden Grove, CA.
8. Leslie Weatherhead. *Life Begins at Death.* (Nashville: Abingdon Press, 1960), p. 23.

SUGGESTED READINGS

BOOKS

Albom, Mitch. *tuesdays with Morrie.* New York: Bantam Doubleday, 1997.

Bach, Marcus. *The Will To Believe.* Los Angeles: Science of Mind Publications, 1988.

Barker, Raymond Charles. *Spirit, Soul and Body.* New York: Barker Associates, 1977.

Becker, Ernest. *The Denial of Death.* New York: The Free Press, 1973.

Berman, Phillip L. *The Journey Home: What Near-Death Experiences and Mysticism Teach Us About the Gift of Life.* New York: Simon & Schuster, 1996.

Buber, Martin. *Tales of the Hasidim: The Early Masters.* New York: Schocken Books, 1975.

____. *A Believing Humanism: My Testament.* New Jersey: Humanities Press International, 1990.

Bynum, Caroline Walker. *The Resurrection of the Body.* New York: Columbia University Press, 1995.

Capra, Fritjof. *The Tao of Physics.* Berkeley: Shambala, 1975.

Chardin, Teilhard de. *The Divine Milieu.* New York: Harper Collins, 1976.

Cruden, Alexander. *Cruden's Complete Concordance of the Old and New Testament.* Grand Rapids: Zondervan Publishing, 1967.

Dass, Ram. *Grist for the Mill.* Berkeley: Celestial Arts, 1988.

Davidson, Glen W. *Living With Dying.* Minneapolis: Augsburg, 1975.

Davis, Stephen T. *Risen Indeed: Making Sense of the Resurrection.* Grand Rapids: W. B. Eerdmans, 1993.

Devers, Edie, Ph.D. *Goodbye Again: Experiences With Departed Loved Ones.* Kansas City: Andrews & McMeel, 1997.

Dole, Bob, and Elizabeth Dole. *The Doles: Unlimited Partners.* New York: Simon & Schuster, 1988.

Doore, Gary, Ph.D. (ed.) *What Survives: Contemporary Explorations of Life After Death.* New York: G.P. Putnam's Sons, 1990.

Dossey, Larry, M.D. *Healing Words: The Power of Prayer and the Practice of Medicine.* New York: The Free Press, 1993.

Eadie, Betty J. *Embraced by the Light.* Placerville, CA: Goldleaf Press, 1992.

Eaton, Ephraim Llewellyn, D.D. *Our Friends Immortal: Can We Talk With Them?* Milwaukee: Advocate Publishing Co., 1946.

Eddy, Mary Baker. *Science and Health With Key to the Scriptures.* Boston: The First Church of Christ, Scientist, 1875.

Eliach, Yaffa. *Hasidic Tales of the Holocaust.* New York: Oxford University Press, 1982.

Eppes-Brown, Joseph. *The Sacred Pipe.* Nashville: Ingram, 1989.

Frankl, Viktor. *Man's Search for Meaning.* Boston: Beacon Press, 1992.

Gallup, George, and W. Proctor. *Adventures in Immortality: A Look Beyond the Threshold of Death.* New York: McGraw-Hill, 1982

Gibran, Kahil. *The Prophet.* Maryland: Alfred A. Knopf, 1976.

Gittelson, Bernard. *Intangible Evidence.* New York: Simon & Schuster, 1987.

Gottschell, A. H. *Dying Words.* England, 1888.

Graham, Billy. *Angels: God's Secret Agents.* Garden City: Doubleday & Co., 1975.

_____. *Facing Death and The Life After.* Minneapolis: Grason, 1987.

Greaves, Helen. *Testimony of Light.* Walden, England: Neville Spearman Publishers, 1985.

Greeley, Andrew. *Death and Beyond.* Chicago: Thomas More Press, 1976.

Grof, Stanislav. *Beyond Death.* New York: Thames & Hudson, 1980.

_____. *Books of the Dead.* New York: Thames & Hudson, 1994.

_____. *The Holotropic Mind.* San Francisco: Harper & Row, 1992.

Guggenheim, Bill, and Judy Guggenheim. *Hello From Heaven.* New York: Bantam, 1996.

Harman, Willis, Ph.D., and Howard Rheingold. *Higher Creativity: Liberating the Unconscious for Breakthrough Insights.* New York: Putnam, 1984.

Hastings, Arthur. *With the Tongues of Men and Angels: A Study of Channeling.* Ft. Worth: Holt, Rinehart & Winston, 1991.

Heschel, Abraham. *God in Search of Man.* New York: Farrar, Strauss, Giroux, 1976.

Heywood, Rosalind. *Beyond the Reach of Sense.* New York: E. P. Dutton & Co., 1961.

Hick, John. *Death and Eternal Life.* Kentucky: John Knox Press, 1994.

Hulst, Dorothy J. *As a Woman Thinketh.* California: DeVorss & Co., 1910.

Israel, Martin, M.D., Rev. *Life Eternal.* Cambridge: Cowley Publishers, 1993.

_____. *Happiness That Lasts.* New York: Cassell, 1999.

_____. *The Dark Face of Reality.* New York: HarperCollins, 1989.

Jones, Alan. *The Soul's Journey: Exploring the Three Passages of the Spiritual Life with Dante as a Guide.* San Francisco: Harper & Row, 1995.

Karlis, Osis, and Erlendur Haraldsson. *At the Hour of Death.* New York: Avon, 1977.

Keller, Phillip. *Inspirational Writings of Phillip Keller: A Shepherd Looks at the Good Shepherd and His Sheep.* New York: Inspiration Press, 1993.

Kelsey, Morton. *Afterlife: The Other Side of Dying.* New York: Paulist Press, 1979.

Kreeft, Peter. *Everything You Ever Wanted To Know About Heaven.* New York: Harper & Row, 1982.

_____. *Heaven: The Heart's Deepest Longing.* San Francisco: Ignatius Press, 1989.

Krishnamurti, J. *On God.* San Francisco: Harper & Row, 1992.

_____. *The Wholeness of Life.* San Francisco: Harper & Row, 1979.

Kübler-Ross, Elisabeth. *On Life After Death.* Berkeley: Celestial Arts, 1991.

LaGrand, Louis E., Ph.D. *After-Death Communication: Extraordinary Experiences of Those Mourning the Death of Loved Ones.* St. Paul: Llewellyn Publishers, 1997.

Larson, Bruce. Ph.D. *The Presence: The God Who Delivers and Guides.* San Francisco: Harper & Row, 1990.

LeShan, Lawrence, Ph.D. *The Medium, the Mystic, and the Physicist: Toward a General Theory of the Paranormal.* New York: Viking, 1974.

_____. *How To Meditate.* New York: Bantam-Doubleday, 1975.

Levine, Stephen. *Who Dies?* New York: Doubleday, 1982.

_____. *Healing Into Life and Death.* New York: Doubleday, 1987.

Lewis, C.S. *The Great Divorce.* New York: Collier Books, 1946.

_____. *The Last Battle.* New York: Macmillan, 1956.

_____. *Screwtape Letters.* New York: Macmillan, 1943.

_____. *The Problem of Pain.* New York: Simon & Schuster, 1996.

_____. *A Grief Observed.* New York: HarperCollins, 1961.

MacDonald, Gordon. *The Life That God Blesses: Weathering the Storms of Life That Threaten the Soul.* Nashville: Thomas Nelson, 1994.

Maguire, Daniel C. *Death By Choice.* Garden City: Image Books, 1984.

_____. *The Moral Revolution: A Christian Humanist Vision.* San Francisco: Harper & Row, 1986.

Martin, Joel, and Patricia Romanowski. *Love Beyond Life: The Healing Power of After-Death Communication.* New York: HarperCollins, 1997.

_____. *Our Children Forever.* New York: Berkley Books,1994.

_____. *We Don't Die: George Anderson's Conversations with the Other Side.* New York: Berkley Books, 1988.

McDonell, Colleen, and Bernhard Lang. *Heaven: A History.* New Haven: Yale University Press, 1990.

Meek, George W. *After We Die, What Then?* Columbus, OH: Ariel Press, 1987.

Millen, Peggy Tabor. *Mary's Way.* Berkeley: Celestial Arts, 1991.

Moody, Raymond A., M.D. *The Light Beyond.* New York: Bantam, 1998.

Morse, Melvin, M.D. *Closer To the Light: Learning From the Near Death Experiences of Children.* New York: Ivy Books, 1990.

_____. *Parting Visions.* New York: Villard Books, 1994.

Myers, John. *Voices from the Edge of Eternity.* Uhrichsville, OH: Barbour & Co., 1968.

Myss, Caroline, Ph.D. *Anatomy of the Spirit.* New York: Crown, 1997.

———. *Why People Don't Heal and How They Can.* New York: Three Rivers Press, 1997.

Nieman, Carol and Emily Goldman. *Afterlife: The Complete Guide to Life After Death.* New York: Viking Studio Books, 1994.

Nouwen, Henri. *Beyond the Mirror: Reflections on Life and Death.* New York: Crossroad, 1990.

Oppenheimer, Helen. *The Hope of Heaven: What Happens When We Die?* Cincinnati: Forward Movement Publications, 1988.

Peale, Norman Vincent. *The Power of Positive Thinking.* New York: Prentice Hall Press, 1987.

———. *The Healing of Sorrow.* Norwalk, CT: C. R. Gibson Co., 1966.

Peck, M. Scott. *People of the Lie.* New York: Simon & Schuster, Inc., 1983.

Piburn, Sidney (ed). *The Dalai Lama: A Policy of Kindness.* Ithaca: Snow Lion Publications, 1993.

Pike, James A., with Diane Kennedy. *The Other Side.* New York: Doubleday, 1968.

Pole, Tudor. *The Silent Road.* London: Neville Spearman, 1960.

Raphael Simcha, Paul. *Jewish Views of the Afterlife.* New York: Jason Aronson, 1995.

Rauscher, William V. *The Spiritual Frontier.* New York: Doubleday, 1975.

Redfield, James. *The Celestine Prophecy.* New York: Time Warner, 1993.

Rinpoche, Sogyal. *The Tibetan Book of Living and Dying.* San Francisco: HarperSanFrancisco, 1993.

Ring, Kenneth. *Heading Toward Omega: In Search of the Meaning of Near Death Experiences.* New York: William Morrow, 1985.

———. *Life At Death: A Scientific Investigation of Near Death Experience.* New York: Coward, McCann & Geoghegan, 1980.

Ritchie, George, M.D. *Ordered to Return: My Life After Dying.* Charlottesville, VA: Hampton Roads Publishing, 1998

———. *Return from Tomorrow.* Grand Rapids: S.H. Revell, 1994.

Russell, Robert A. *Dry Those Tears.* Marina Del Ray, CA: DeVorss, 1986.

Schaffer, Ulrich. *Surprised by Light.* New York: Harper & Row, 1980.

Schuller, Robert. *Positive Encouragement For You! 365 Promises of Hope from the Heart of God.* Garden Grove, CA: Robert Schuller, 1988.

Schwarz, Hans. *Beyond The Gates of Death: A Biblical Examination of Evidence For Life After Death.* Minneapolis: Augsburg Publishing, 1981.

Sharp, Anne Wallace, and Susan Handle Terbay. *Gifts: Two Hospice Professionals Reveal Messages From Those Passing On.* NJ: New Horizon Press, 1997.

Sherman, Doug, and William Hendricks. *Your Work Matters to God.* Colorado Springs: NavPress, 1987.

Siegel, Bernie, M.D. *Love, Medicine, and Miracles.* New York: Harper & Row, 1986.

Simcox, Carroll E. *The Eternal You: An Exploration of a Spiritual Intuition.* New York: Crossroad, 1986.

Simon, Sidney B., and Suzanne Simon. *Forgiveness: How To Make Peace with Your Past and Get On with Your Life.* New York: Warner Books, 1990.

Stanley, Charles. *Eternal Security: Can You Be Sure?* Nashville: Thomas Nelson, Inc., 1990.

Steiger, Brad, and Sherry Hansen Steiger. *Children of the Light.* New York: Signet, 1995.

Strommen, Merton P., and A. Irene Strommen. *Five Cries of Grief.* New York: HarperCollins, 1993.

Swedenborg, Emmanuel. *Heaven and Its Wonders and Hell.* New York: Swedenborg Foundation, 1940.

Synnestvedt, Sig. *The Essential Swedenborg.* New York: Twayne, 1970.

Tada, Joni Eareckson. *Heaven: Your Real Home.* Grand Rapids, MI: Zondervan, 1995.

Treece, Patricia. *Messengers: After-Death Appearances of Saints and Mystics.* Huntington, IN: Our Sunday Visitor, 1995.

Turner, Alice K. *The History of Hell.* New York: Harcourt Brace, 1993.

Underhill, Elizabeth. *Mysticism.* New York: Crossroad, 1960.

Vardey, Lucinda (ed). *God In All Worlds.* New York: Vintage, 1995.

Vaughan, Frances E. *Awakening Intuition.* New York: Anchor Books/Doubleday, 1979.

Weatherhead, Leslie D. *Life Begins At Death.* Nashville: Abingdon Press, 1969.

_____. *The Will of God.* New York: Cokesbury, 1944.

Weiner, Herbert. *9½ Mystics: The Kabbala Today.* New York: Macmillan, 1992.

Wesley, John. *Little Instruction Book: A Classic Treasury of Timeless Wisdom and Reflection.* Tulsa: Honor Books, 1996.

Wilson, Colin. *Afterlife: An Investigation of the Evidence for Life After Death.* Garden City, NY, Doubleday, 1987.

Wilson, Ian. *The After Death Experience: The Physics of the Non-Physical.* New York: William Morrow, 1987.

Zaleski, Carol. *The Life of the World to Come: New Death Experience and Christian Hope.* New York: Oxford University Press, 1996.

_____. *Otherworld Journeys: Accounts of Near-Death Experiences in Medieval Times.* New York: Oxford University Press, 1987.

Zukav, Gary. *The Seat of the Soul.* New York: Simon & Schuster, 1989.

PERIODICALS

Bradley, Rose Ann. "A Child's View of Heaven." *Marriage and Family Living.* August 1987, pp. 17–18.

Greeley, Andrew. "Correlates of Belief in Life After Death." *Sociology and Social Research* 71 (July 1987): 3–8.

Lorrimer, David. "New Death Experiences and Ethical Transformation." *Noetic Science Review.* Winter 1994, p. 39.

Rhine, J. B. "The Reality of the Spirit." *Guideposts.* September 1963, pp. 10–11.

Sagan, Carl. "In the Valley of the Shadow." *Parade Magazine.* March 10, 1996, pp. 18–21.

ABOUT THE AUTHOR

Jacquelyn Frances Oliveira, M.A., is a consultant and Director of Grief Education and Counseling at Wisconsin Memorial Park in Brookfield, Wisconsin.

She designs and conducts monthly programs for the public, counsels individuals and families, and facilitates two Healing Beyond Loss support groups at the Park each week. Ms. Oliveira is a Nationally Certified Death Educator and Grief Counselor.

From 1975 to 1981 she directed two federally funded Title 1 Higher Education Programs in metropolitan Milwaukee: Widowed Persons Service, and Crisis, Change, Recovery for Middle-Aged Adults.

She has been a college educator for 20 years in the Social Sciences and has served as a consultant and grief recovery group facilitator at a Milwaukee funeral home for 11 years. Ms. Oliveira is currently an instructor at Marquette University in the Certificate in Grief Support Program.